Teddy Roosevelt & Leonard Wood

Teddy Roosevelt & Leonard Wood

PARTNERS IN COMMAND

John S. D. Eisenhower

UNIVERSITY OF MISSOURI PRESS COLUMBIA

University of Missouri Press, Columbia, Missouri 65201
Printed and bound in the United States of America

5 4 3 2 1 18 17 16 15 14

Cataloging-in-Publication data available from the Library of Congress
ISBN 978-0-8262-2000-4

∞™ This paper meets the requirements of the
American National Standard for Permanence of Paper
for Printed Library Materials, Z39.48, 1984.

Design and composition: Jennifer Cropp
Printing and binding: Thomson–Shore, Inc.
Typeface: Minion

To Mitchell Yockelson

Contents

Cuba and the Caribbean, 1898
0 50 100 Kilometers
0 50 100 Miles
UNITED STATES
Gulf of Mexico
Straits of Florida
Atlantic Ocean
The Bahamas (U.K.)
Havana
PINAR DEL RIO
SANTA CLARA
Yucatan Channel
ISLE OF PINES
PUERTO PRINCIPLE
SANTIAGO DE CUBA
Santiago
Guantánamo
Caribbean Sea
Landing at Daiquiri
Landing at Guantánamo
Windward Passage
Cayman Islands (U.K.)
Jamaica (U.K.)
HAITI
Map by Chris Robinson

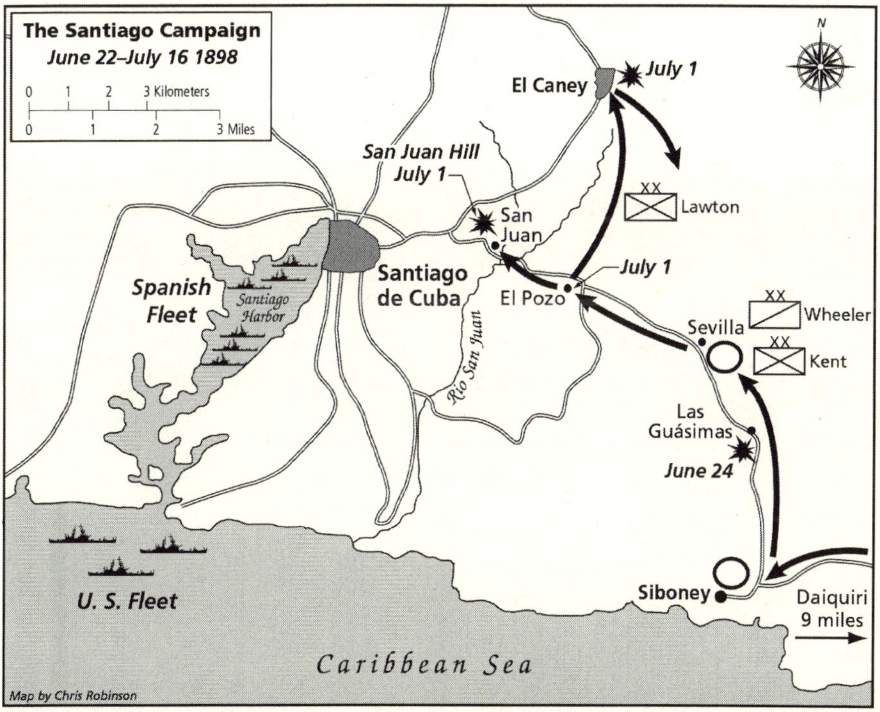
The Santiago Campaign
June 22–July 16 1898
0 1 2 3 Kilometers
0 1 2 3 Miles
N
El Caney
July 1
San Juan Hill
July 1
San Juan
Lawton
Spanish Fleet
Santiago Harbor
Santiago de Cuba
El Pozo
July 1
Sevilla
Wheeler
Kent
Rio San Juan
Las Guásimas
June 24
U. S. Fleet
Siboney
Daiquiri 9 miles
Caribbean Sea
Map by Chris Robinson

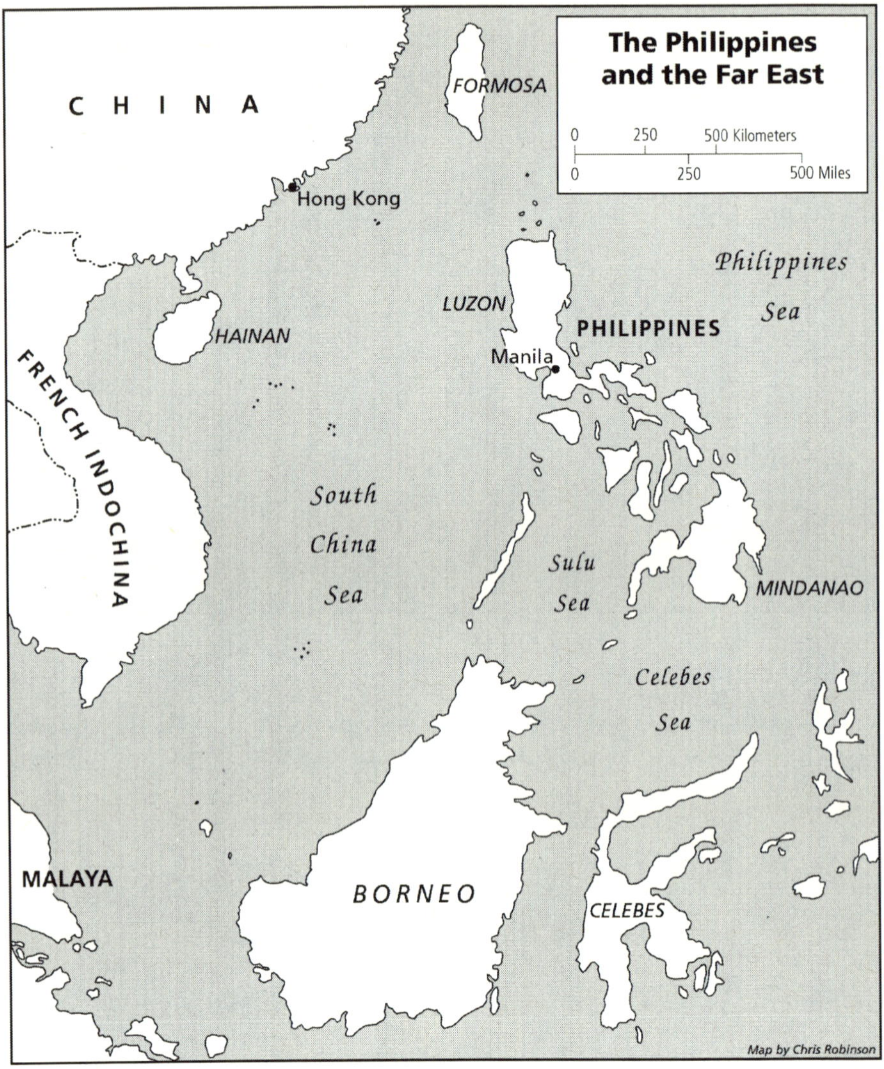
The Philippines and the Far East
0 250 500 Kilometers
0 250 500 Miles
CHINA
Hong Kong
FORMOSA
HAINAN
LUZON
PHILIPPINES
Manila
Philippines Sea
FRENCH INDOCHINA
South China Sea
Sulu Sea
MINDANAO
Celebes Sea
BORNEO
CELEBES
MALAYA
Map by Chris Robinson

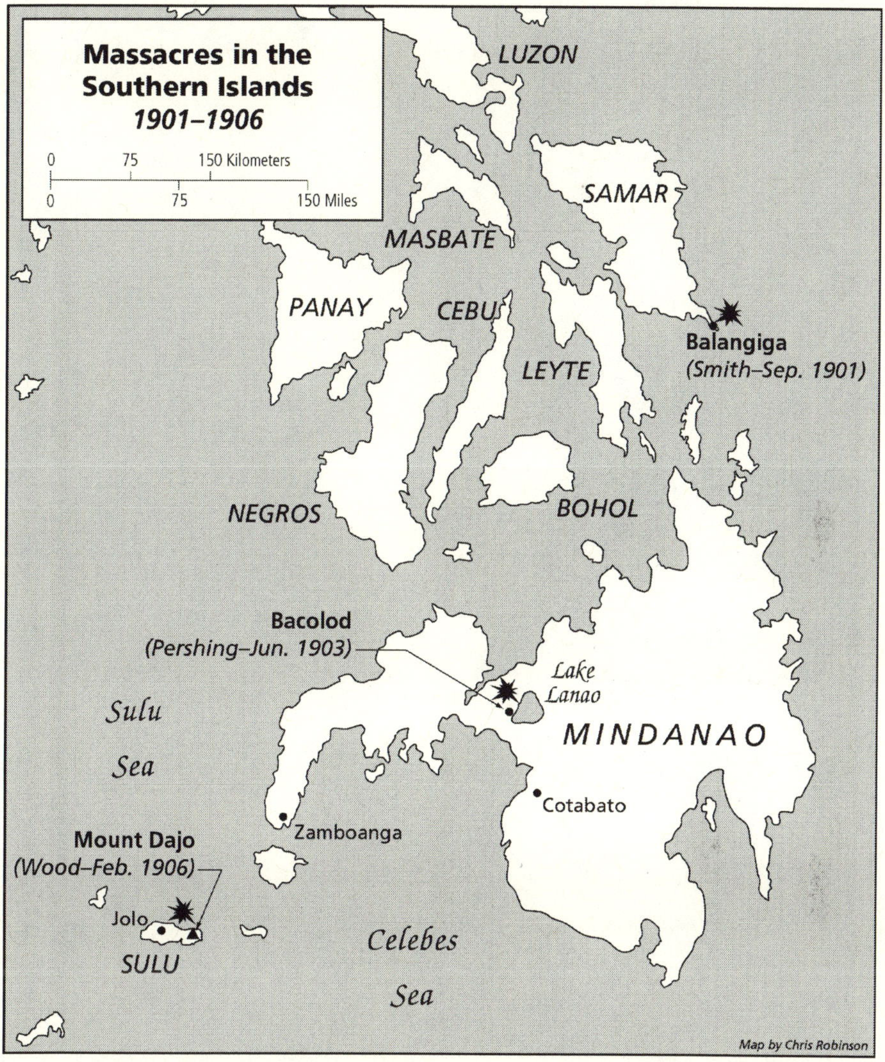
Massacres in the Southern Islands
1901–1906
0
75
150 Kilometers
0
75
150 Miles
LUZON
SAMAR
MASBATE
PANAY
CEBU
LEYTE
Balangiga
(Smith–Sep. 1901)
NEGROS
BOHOL
Bacolod
(Pershing–Jun. 1903)
Lake Lanao
MINDANAO
Sulu Sea
Cotabato
Zamboanga
Mount Dajo
(Wood–Feb. 1906)
Jolo
SULU
Celebes Sea
Map by Chris Robinson

Teddy Roosevelt & Leonard Wood

Introduction

This is the story not of two men, but of a friendship, an association. President Theodore Roosevelt and General Leonard Wood, two remarkable men, were the leading proponents of American strength and power during the first two decades of the twentieth century. Greatly different in personality, they shared an obsession with the role of war in the promotion of a glorious American destiny. They went so far as to believe in the benefits of war itself.

Though highly influential at the time, their partnership has been forgotten or at least relegated to the memories of soldiers and military historians. Roosevelt has been remembered for his heroic action at the Battle of San Juan Hill, Cuba, as part of the 1898 Spanish–American War, but few remember that he served under Wood. The Rough Riders, formally known as the 1st United States Volunteer Cavalry Regiment, fought bravely, though overblown by the prose of reporter Richard Harding Davis. Other regiments contributed as much to that victory, perhaps more, but to the public, the name "San Juan Hill" belongs to Teddy Roosevelt.

The United States easily defeated Spain in the so–called "splendid little war,"[1] but success was achieved principally because of the weakness of the Spanish, who were by now a third–rate power. The American expeditions were full of confusion. Supplies, transportation, proper food, training, and even modern rifles were missing. Thus, when Roosevelt became president of the United States in 1901, one of his goals was to reorganize the Army and the Navy, particularly the Army. Aided by that most capable secretary of war, Elihu Root, he set out to rectify organizational evils under which the Army had suffered throughout its history. Never one to forget his friends and allies, TR also arranged for Wood, a Regular Army captain in the Medical Corps, to keep his wartime rank of major general.

As a young general, jumping over hundreds of more senior officers, Wood justified the president's confidence. After serving as governor of Cuba and

1. John Hay, American ambassador to London.

later the Moro Province of the Philippines, he was appointed Army chief of staff under President William H. Taft in 1910. There his drive was indispensable. Although TR and Root had set the organizational groundwork for a modern "progressive" army on paper, the implementation of their changes had met passive resistance from the conservatives, especially the technical services, and little had been done until the arrival of Wood. He possessed the strength necessary to put real teeth in Roosevelt's reorganization. He made Roosevelt's changes actually work.

The final achievement of this partnership was the most important, the leadership of the so–called Preparedness Movement in the days before the American participation in the Great War. The War Department hierarchy had been restructured, but to protect itself against threats from without, the United States needed troops. Even before the outbreak of the European war in August 1914, TR and Wood were painfully conscious of how weak the Army was, its mobile combat force limited to about twenty thousand troops, in contrast to millions in the armies of Europe. Even after the war broke out, the United States still failed to react in any noticeable manner. By then Wood was no longer chief of staff, but he was still commander of the Army's all–important Eastern Department, and in that post he was able to do much. With former president Roosevelt's enthusiastic support—and President Woodrow Wilson's tolerance—Wood founded the great training program, the first and most noted camp being at Plattsburg, New York.[2] His pioneering in training young officers—sniffingly but unfairly called "ninety–day wonders"—produced the critical corps of young officers who did so much to provide leadership when the United States was drawn into the conflict in 1917.

Unfortunately, the Preparedness Movement ran counter to the policies of President Wilson, who regarded the act of expanding the Army as a threat to his ambition to appear on the world stage as a peacemaker. To make matters worse, the public statements of both Roosevelt and Wood were no help in winning Wilson's support. Roosevelt, who showed contempt for Wilson's "neutrality," made personal remarks about the president's moral and even physical courage. Wood's jeremiads were more restrained, but they still went beyond the limit of what was generally considered proper for an officer in uniform. Wilson took these attacks with remarkable equanimity, but he exacted his revenge when the United States entered the war. He denied both Wood

2. The city of Plattsburgh has since added an *h* to the end of the name. In 1915, however, the correct spelling was Plattsburg, the spelling that will be used here.

and Roosevelt their heart's desire, the opportunity to go to France and participate in the war against the kaiser's Imperial Germany.

On the personal side, the friendship between president and general was deep, even though they were in early middle age when they first met at a Washington social event in 1897. Roosevelt, at forty years of age, was the elder by two years; furthermore, he was already a national figure, the assistant secretary of the Navy; Wood, on the other hand, was only a captain in the Army Medical Corps, albeit personal physician to President William McKinley. It required all of TR's influence in high places to induce Secretary of War Russell Alger to permit the organization of the Rough Riders in 1898. But Roosevelt was cognizant of his own military limitations, and he insisted that Wood should be the colonel of the regiment, with Roosevelt serving under him as his lieutenant colonel.

Once in uniform, however, Wood was Roosevelt's unquestioned boss for those few months of 1898, despite the public's perception of their unit as "Roosevelt's Rough Riders." At the end of the Cuban campaign, when Roosevelt left, their intimate service together came to an end. But their intimacy survived. Throughout the rest of their lives, they acted as if there were no gap in seniority between them. Wood was not above speaking his mind in their correspondence. Once at least he even mildly chastised the president when the latter seemed to renege on what Wood had considered an understanding.

Neither man was prone to introspection, and the way they regarded themselves individually has an amusing aspect. Roosevelt, the master politician, liked to think of himself primarily as a soldier; he insisted on being addressed as "Colonel" even after leaving the presidency. Yet TR would have been a disastrous Regular Army officer, for the all–important quality of discipline was not in him. By contrast, Wood, a first–rate soldier, grew to regard himself as a capable politician. In fact, he was nearly as ineffective in that area as his great forebear Winfield Scott, in the first half of the nineteenth century.

Although both TR and Wood were denied the overseas wartime experience they craved, neither considered himself finished on the public scene when the war was over. Setting military matters aside, they turned their eyes toward the future of the Republican Party in 1920, encouraged by the unpopularity of Wilson's Democrats. Their hopes for Roosevelt to run for president in 1920 came to a halt, however, when Roosevelt died unexpectedly in early–January 1919, just short of his sixtieth birthday.

Even in death, however, the two friends remained a team. At the behest of the Roosevelt family—a mandate much to his own liking—Wood assumed the role of Roosevelt as the front runner for the Republican presidential nomination in 1920. Inheriting the support of the Roosevelt faction, he went to the Republican convention in Chicago with more delegates pledged to him than any of the other presidential hopefuls. Predictably, however, he failed miserably. Sensing that the party conservatives were coming back to power, he abandoned Roosevelt's progressive principles in favor of the conservative. He was a poor salesman. The convention spurned him and turned instead to Warren G. Harding.

Leonard Wood had a few more years of useful service ahead of him even after Roosevelt's death and his own political defeat, but his greatest claim to fame had been established as a partner of his old Rough Rider, Theodore Roosevelt.

1

The Birth of a Friendship

One evening in late-June 1897, Theodore Roosevelt and Leonard Wood met at a stag party in Washington. Their paths may or may not have crossed before—they were both visible men on the Washington scene—but this was the first time they took real notice of each other. In their own ways, they were both important men. Roosevelt, as the assistant secretary of the Navy, far outranked Wood, who was only a captain in the Army Medical Corps. But Wood was no ordinary medical officer; he was the personal physician to President William McKinley. As such, he was the man who presumably had the president's ear. Despite the disparity in their ranks, therefore, no gap in status stood between them.

For some mysterious reason—call it chemistry—Roosevelt and Wood bonded instantly. At the end of the evening's event, therefore, they decided to walk home together. The distances were not great and the weather pleasant. As they talked, they discovered that they shared personal characteristics. Both were highly ambitious, and both were dedicated to physical strength and vitality. Roosevelt was impressed by Wood's manliness. Tall and muscular, he walked at an extremely fast pace, easily outdistancing Roosevelt, who had taken pride in the speed with which he could cover the streets of New York as police commissioner. Roosevelt was also aware of Wood's distinguished record in battle against the Apache chieftain Geronimo ten years earlier. In light of Roosevelt's mind-set, it is not surprising that he, though two years older, developed something of a hero worship for Wood.

Aside from personal compatibility, however, the two men thought alike regarding the burning issue of the day: the current Caribbean crisis. There the Cubans, who had suffered under Spanish rule for about three centuries, had finally risen in rebellion. The recently appointed Spanish governor, Valeriano

Weyler, had just established a set of concentration camps, and it was estimated that three hundred thousand rebels were incarcerated in these closed-off areas. It was reported that as many as one hundred thousand had died.[1] The question was, what role should the United States play?

The public at that time was divided on the issue. Most Americans were probably inclined to a hands-off policy. Some, however, were now beginning to feel that the United States had an obligation for a military intervention. Goaded on by two newspaper magnates, William Randolph Hearst and Joseph Pulitzer, the issue was becoming a topic of intense discussion.

It is not surprising that Roosevelt and Wood viewed this situation alike, because both were ardent expansionists whose imperialist ambitions reached even beyond the Cuban situation. Both, for example, were foreseeing an occupation of the Hawaiian Islands far beyond the elimination of Spain from all the Caribbean. The construction of a canal across Central America to join the Atlantic and Pacific was still in the future.

By the time the two men reached their respective destinations, an association, both an alliance and a friendship, had been born.

1. David F. Trask, *The War with Spain in 1898*, 9.

2

Sagamore Cowboy, Theodore Roosevelt

Though Roosevelt and Wood had much in common, their personalities were quite different. Roosevelt was ebullient, loquacious, even frenetic by nature; Wood, though no recluse, was relatively reserved, as befitted his New England birth and upbringing. Roosevelt was a politician whose success depended on the success with which he promoted himself. Wood, as part of the established military society, knew his place and kept it. Neither man could change, and neither had any desire to do so.

Theodore Roosevelt was born on October 27, 1858, in New York City, the first son and second child of Theodore Roosevelt Sr. and Martha Bulloch Roosevelt.[1] Although the name Roosevelt is automatically associated with privilege, the members of Theodore's branch of the family, in contrast to Franklin's, were not very wealthy; they had to work to maintain their comfortable standard of living. The elder Theodore Roosevelt made a good living as a glass importer and later as a banker. The family loved the outdoors and spent as much time as possible at their weekend retreat at Oyster Bay, Long Island. The father also owned property in what was then the Dakota Territories. Zeal for the wide–open spaces never left young Theodore Roosevelt.

As a child, young Theodore Roosevelt was afflicted with serious asthma, which made him sickly. For that and other reasons, he was educated at home until he entered Harvard in 1876 at the age of eighteen. He was, however, energetic, curious, and determined, far from subdued by his malady. He played sports with zest. He also developed a strong interest in nature,

1. It is easy to confuse the names, because the son and future president was born a junior. He dropped the "junior" on his father's death.

especially ornithology. He seemed to need physical activity. Professor Aloysius Norton describes one incident that occurred when Theodore was at Harvard University: "While skating on Fresh Pond with [Harvard] classmate Richard Welling on a bitter winter day, Roosevelt went endlessly round and round. Welling from boyhood had accepted heavy weather as a challenge, but this day was just too much for him. When Roosevelt shouted, 'Isn't this bully?' Welling could only wonder. He later commented, 'It puzzled me how this youngster who had not my health, for he was asthmatic, and he not my muscle, could want more of that winter gale.'"[2]

The elder Roosevelt exercised an unusual influence on his son. The boy respected and loved his opinionated mother, a belle who had never accepted the defeat of the South in the Civil War, but it was his father to whom young Theodore looked for guidance. One dark spot of his father's past haunted the boy, however. Theodore was aware that his father had avoided service in the Civil War by hiring a substitute.

At Harvard, Roosevelt stood high in his class, high enough to be invited to join Phi Beta Kappa on graduation. However, he seems to have made no effort to reach the very top. Unfortunately, his father died during his sophomore year, and his grief was almost overwhelming. It has been said that the anguish stemming from that loss hardened him to face later similar experiences. He would have his full share of them.

Roosevelt never regarded his experience at Harvard as one that had done much for him, and he may have been right; formal academics had never enchanted him. But the period was significant for the outside activities he participated in. He made hunting and fishing trips to Maine, where his zest for the outdoors was whetted and where he came in contact with many working men. Perhaps to his surprise, he found himself to be completely comfortable with them. His respect for the "ordinary" people stayed with Roosevelt all his life.

In early 1879, while he was visiting family friends in Cambridge, Roosevelt met a young lady named Alice Lee. Immediately taken by her, he quickly resolved to make her his wife. She, however, was not so sure. During his entire senior year at Harvard, Theodore wooed her ardently but without success. Finally, he determined to bring matters to a head; he demanded that she marry him and made it clear that if she refused, he would seek a wife elsewhere. Alice, realizing that it was now or never, dropped her coy attitude and consented. They were married in October 1880.

Just a few days before his marriage to Alice Lee, Theodore Roosevelt entered Columbia University Law School. But his enrollment did not mean that he

2. Aloysius A. Norton, *Theodore Roosevelt,* 18.

would spend his honeymoon poring over law books. In the somewhat relaxed world of the day, the couple visited Europe, and when they returned to New York Roosevelt entered politics while still a law student. It happened almost by chance. Roosevelt's friends nominated him to run on the Republican ticket for the position of assemblyman from New York's Twenty–First District. His acceptance of the nomination met with some protests from relatives, who considered the position of assemblyman beneath the family dignity. In November, much to his amazement, he was elected. He was still only twenty–three.

Those were busy times for Roosevelt. In addition to his duties as an assemblyman, which he performed conscientiously, he also found time to write a book, *The Naval War of 1812.* His voracious reading had convinced him that all previous treatments of the subject had been inaccurate and needed revision. It was a huge success. A few years after its publication, when Roosevelt met Captain Alfred Thayer Mahan, the celebrated naval strategist, Roosevelt's enemies sniffed that he had stolen some of Mahan's ideas. They were misguided: Roosevelt's book had come out earlier than Mahan's.

As an assemblyman from a prominent family, Roosevelt and his wife were much involved in New York society. Robert Lincoln, son of President Abraham Lincoln and a successful man in his own right, introduced the couple to such luminaries as writer Henry James, author Edward Everett Hale, and Lieutenant General Irvin McDowell, whose defeat as the Union commander at the Battle of Bull Run twenty years earlier had not prevented his being a social celebrity.

On February 14, 1884, this happy life came to an abrupt end. By incredible coincidence, Roosevelt's mother and his beloved Alice both died on the same day and in the same house, Alice leaving Roosevelt with an infant daughter. Roosevelt's grief was overpowering. He wrote in his diary, "The light has gone out of my life."[3] He went into a state of physical shock, and for a few days he remained nearly unconscious of reality.

Nothing, however, could hold Theodore Roosevelt down for long. He soon began to recover from his grief. Two months later, in April 1884, he wrote to the editor of a Utica newspaper, "Although not a very old man, I have lived a great deal of my life, and I have known sorrow too bitter and joy too keen to allow me to become either cast down or elated for more than a very brief period over any successes or defeats."[4]

At the end of his term as a New York assemblyman, Roosevelt chose not to run for reelection. He was now attaining a national reputation because of a

3. H. W. Brands, *T. R.: The Last Romantic,* 162.

4. Roosevelt to Simon Newton Dexter North, April 30, 1884, cited in ibid., 24.

civil service bill he had pushed through the assembly, and he was noted even more for the enthusiastic reception of *The Naval War of 1812.* He therefore left his infant daughter, Alice, with his sister Anna and took to the outdoors at his properties near Medora, Dakota Territory. He went not to assuage his grief, but because he was bored with the routine of his life in New York.

Roosevelt's couple of years in the Dakotas constituted a significant period. He was not skilled as a rancher—shooting, roping, and riding—but he put such effort into his work that he managed to build his once frail body into a strong one, a continuing process. He mixed well with his three hands, who lived with him in a two–story cabin he called Maltese Cross Ranch. In 1884, after staying a year at Maltese Cross, he bought another, more elaborate, establishment that he called Elkhorn, on the Little Missouri River. He had no intention of being a serious farmer, but he bought a herd of a thousand cattle for the sum of twenty–six thousand dollars and went on hunting expeditions in the Badlands, especially along the Little Missouri River.

He also took on the chore of local sheriff, in which his most noted exploit was to track down three men who had stolen his boat on the Little Missouri. By vigilante law, he could have hanged them, but he chose instead to deliver them to Dickinson for trial. He made the trip without assistance from other guards, staying awake for a full forty hours.

Although living with his ranch hands increased Roosevelt's comfort with the "working man," he did not confine his activities to ranching. He traveled back and forth to New York to visit his daughter, Alice, in the meantime building up his political connections. Principal among these new friends was a man who was Roosevelt's senior by eight years, Henry Cabot Lodge, then a representative from Massachusetts.

The close friendship that developed between Roosevelt and Lodge was unusual in that they were poles apart domestically. Lodge was a rock–ribbed Republican conservative; Roosevelt, though also officially a Republican, was instinctively a progressive. What they had in common was that both men were fervid expansionists, a fact that would cement their alliance throughout their lives. Incidentally, both men at that time considered themselves to be primarily authors.[5]

---

5. Roosevelt's main incentive for a sojourn into the wilderness may have been to attain time for writing. During his time in North Dakota, he published a popular book, *The Hunting Trips of a Rancher.* He also amassed material for future books on the West, continuing literary exchanges with Lodge, who had just published a biography of Daniel Webster.

Finally, it was time for Roosevelt to return to New York. Research for historical works was difficult in the Dakotas, a region almost totally lacking in library facilities. His letters included the word *lonely* with increasing frequency. So it was probably without much regret that he accepted the invitation of the Republican Party to run for mayor of New York, even though he knew he never had a chance. After his expected defeat, he retired to Oyster Bay, where he built a home he called Sagamore Hill. Here his writing became serious; the expenses of maintaining that establishment required money, which he earned by writing and speaking. In 1887 he published a biography of Senator Thomas Hart Benton, and the next year he produced a similar work on Gouverneur Morris, one of the founders of the Republic. Incredibly, in the same year, he produced another book on the West, *Ranch Life and the Hunting Trail.*

Roosevelt now reentered the mainstream of life. In November 1886, he surprised his friends by announcing that he was off to London to marry Miss Edith Kermit Carow, a childhood sweetheart with whom he had never completely lost contact. Thus began a marriage that produced a daughter and four sons. In 1889, when the Republicans regained the presidency under Benjamin Harrison, Roosevelt was appointed to be Civil Service commissioner. It was a natural choice; Roosevelt's sponsorship of the bill establishing the Civil Service Commission in New York had not been forgotten. He served in that post for six years, including two under Grover Cleveland when the Democrats regained the White House in the 1892 election. (The Civil Service was not subject to partisan politics at that time.)

Cleveland was sensible in retaining the services of this Republican, because he was extremely effective. As Roosevelt boasted in his autobiography, "During my six years' service as Commissioner in the field, the merit system was extended at the expense of the spoils system so as to include several times the number of offices that had originally been included. Generally this was done by the introduction of competitive entrance examinations; sometimes, as in the Navy–Yards, by a system of registration. This of itself was good work."[6]

Roosevelt claimed other achievements, of course, but the position was not challenging. Its greatest advantage was that it produced enough free time that he could pursue his main passion: writing. During his six years, he wrote and published three books.

By the end of that time, Roosevelt was once more becoming restless, and he gladly accepted the post of police commissioner for the City of New York.

6. Theodore Roosevelt, *An Autobiography,* 137.

There, though he stayed only a couple of years, the time was exceedingly active and productive.

It was not an easy position. Just at the time Roosevelt was sworn in, the mayor, William L. Strong, reorganized the Police Board to include two Republicans and two Democrats, with each member empowered with a veto to negate the acts of all four. In addition, the police chief, who served under the board, enjoyed an unusual degree of latitude in his own right. The Police Department was notoriously sloppy and undisciplined, the worst difficulties being with the widespread practice of accepting bribes.

That largely rectified, Roosevelt faced other frustrations. One was his futile effort to enforce the city ordinance against Sunday drinking in public places. It was not motivated by a disapproval of drinking on Roosevelt's part, but he intended to enforce the law. Theretofore, saloon keepers had avoided enforcement of the law by slipping a little cash under the table to the police. Roosevelt succeeded in stopping the bribery, but he lost his battle against the booze. The saloon keepers cited a city ordinance that allowed liquor with meals. When a judge ruled that seventeen beers with a pretzel constituted a "meal," Roosevelt knew he was defeated.

There were other facets to this assignment, however. Roosevelt continued his friendship with the reformer Jacob Riis, and in the course of roaming the back precincts of the city, he was struck by the plight of the poor, thus enhancing his natural tendency toward reform. And while he was walking the streets of New York, he continued to build his body by making every walk a speed march. No man could keep up with him until he met Leonard Wood.

Roosevelt's duties as police commissioner were arduous and his hours long. As a result, his writing career dropped off dramatically. Nevertheless, he found time to read the reports of Spanish atrocities in Cuba, and he grew more and more obsessed in favor of an American intervention on that island. Although the matter had nothing to do with his position as police commissioner, he expressed his views loud and clear in public and became known nationally as a leading war hawk.

He also entered national politics. In the presidential campaign of 1896, he took time from his civic duties to campaign strenuously for the election of William McKinley. So effective was he, especially in the West, that McKinley, on the urging of Henry Cabot Lodge and others, appointed him to be assistant secretary of the Navy. Though aware of Roosevelt's reputation as a loose cannon, McKinley was assured by Lodge that the position of assistant secretary was one without power. Roosevelt could make no trouble.

Roosevelt had now reached his immediate goal: a subcabinet position in the federal government. He was thirty–nine years old.

3

Doctor on Horseback, Leonard Wood

Unlike the wealthy Theodore Roosevelt, Leonard Wood came from relatively modest beginnings. But his ambition was just as strong, and in some ways more remarkable.

He was a New Englander, born at Winchester, New Hampshire, on October 9, 1860, only a few weeks before the election of Abraham Lincoln. His father, Charles Jewett Wood, was a struggling young medical student at the time. But in 1862, before receiving his MD, he felt that it was his duty to join the Union army as a "hospital steward" in the 42d Massachusetts Volunteers. Although he spent only about a year in service, it was apparently a grim experience. The men of his unit were riddled with sickness, and Wood himself barely survived. He made no secret of his dislike for war. While in the service, he wrote letters to his wife, sparing her nothing of the grim details. In 1863 he returned home again.[1]

Young Leonard spent his youth in Buzzards Bay, Cape Cod. His father, once he had attained a full–fledged medical degree, made enough money that he was able to send Leonard to a respectable high school at Middleboro, New Hampshire. The father and son seemed to have a good relationship, but Wood did not idolize his father as did TR.

Leonard early showed characteristics that he would retain all his life. A quiet boy, he was not much of a social mixer, but he liked Middleboro and his schoolmates liked him. He was unusually athletic and muscular. A striking feature of his physical appearance was his light, almost white, hair. So blond was he that his biographer Hermann Hagedorn compares him more than once to a "Viking."

1. Hermann Hagedorn, *Leonard Wood, a Biography,* 1:1–11.

Although Leonard had a good record at Middleboro, it appeared that his education would end there; his father lacked the money to afford to send him to college. Keenly interested in the military—not inherited from his father—he applied to both the Naval Academy at Annapolis and the Military Academy at West Point. Unfortunately, however, his father lacked the political influence necessary to attain an appointment at either school. So Leonard decided to follow his father into the medical profession. When the elder Wood died in 1880, the twenty–year–old son applied with success to the Harvard Medical School, paying his way by working, largely as a tutor. He graduated as an MD in 1884 and took up his residency as a doctor, even though he secretly still longed for something more adventurous than a domestic medical practice.

He seems, however, to have become a doctor from a sense of duty; his heart was with the Army. In 1885 a situation in far–off Arizona would change Wood's life forever. The fierce Apache chief Geronimo broke out of the confines of his reservation and with a minority of his tribe went on a rampage. A furious President Grover Cleveland, fed up with the humanitarian policies of General George Crook, replaced him with the truculent and aggressive Brigadier General Nelson A. Miles, with orders to bring Geronimo back dead or alive. In the process of building up Miles's force, a call went out for medical doctors to aid in the effort. Wood eagerly signed up. He could not negotiate an officer's commission, however, and had to accept the status of a civilian "contract surgeon," without formal military rank.

Wood went to Fort Whiffle, Arizona, where he reported to Miles and then was sent to Fort Huachuca. There he took up routine duties for the garrison. Nevertheless, though serving in a medical capacity, Wood always made it clear that his goal was to become a commissioned officer of the line—infantry, cavalry, or artillery. Wood must have performed his duties well, for he was soon noticed by Miles himself, who was currently planning an expedition to capture Geronimo. Miles apparently recognized military qualities in Wood besides those necessary for a mere contract surgeon. He determined that Wood would not be confined to Huachuca but would accompany the forthcoming expedition.

In contrast to Crook's more humanitarian policy of using Apache scouts to keep the Indians quiet, Miles, consistent with the views of President Cleveland, now planned to chase Geronimo with American troops, supplemented by the scouts, of course. Miles's dictate was simple: capture or destroy.

The commander of the expedition was Captain Henry W. Lawton, who had been handpicked by Miles to lead it. A gigantic man of six feet, four inches, he was known to be tough, honest, and fair. Like Miles, Lawton had enlisted early in the Civil War and had risen to the grade of lieutenant colonel, commander of the 30th Indiana Volunteer Regiment. He had fought in twenty–two battles and skirmishes in the West, and at the Battle of Atlanta in 1864 he had been awarded the Medal of Honor for conspicuous gallantry. Promotion in war is often a matter of chance, and Lawton, four years younger than Miles, had not been lucky. When the volunteers were demobilized at the end of the Civil War, he had been forced to accept the lowly rank of second lieutenant in order even to remain in the Regular Army. It had taken him fourteen years, to 1879, to regain even the rank of captain.[2] But he had accepted his lot in order to stay in service.

The pursuit of Geronimo might well be termed a posse rather than a military action. President Grover Cleveland had provided Miles with an astonishing total of five thousand soldiers, from which he could draw any force the countryside could support. Geronimo's band, by contrast, consisted of only about thirty–seven braves and about a hundred women and children. Lawton's force consisted of about sixty highly selected men, infantry, cavalry, and a detachment of Apache scouts. Although Lawton was skeptical of a mere contract surgeon, Wood was somehow assigned as Lawton's second in command. Some of the other members of the expedition, especially the tough, weather–beaten mule skinners, resented Wood, but Miles himself had selected him for the position, and Lawton was more than willing to give Wood his chance.

The reason such a small band of Apache could even hope to elude their pursuers lay in the nature of the terrain. The Sierra Madre mountain range south of Douglas, Arizona, and Agua Priete, Sonora, was strange and difficult. The trails were vague, the heights vast, and the cliffs precipitous. The pursuers were forced to travel single file. Geronimo knew every corner of this god–forsaken country. Lawton's Apache scouts were recognized as indispensable.

The expedition left Fort Huachuca on May 5, 1886, traveling eighteen miles the first day, twenty–four the second, and thirty–seven the third.[3] On the route, Wood made a contribution to our knowledge of its progress by writing frequent letters to his brother Jacob (Jake) back home.

Partly because of his need to establish himself as a soldier and partly because of his natural zeal, Wood took risks that would not have been asked of anyone. At one point, for example, he volunteered to carry a dispatch that Lawton needed delivered to a telegraph station for transmission back to Miles. The gist of the message was that the conditions were much more severe than expected and that the pursuit should be given up. Wood would have to carry the message through perilous territory. Pantano, the telegraph station,

2. Under such conditions, an officer held an honorary position, though not paid, at his highest previous rank.

3. Ibid., 68.

was located about twenty–five miles distant, on a crooked trail, in the darkness. Authorized to take one man with him, he chose an old soldier whom he described as "about used up." According to Wood, "The old soldier played out when about two–thirds of the distance."[4]

Wood made it to Pantano—he never mentioned the fate of the soldier—and awaited Miles's reply to Lawton's message. The answer was quick but disappointing: the general ordered Lawton to continue the pursuit as rapidly as possible and wherever it might lead. Wood was off on his return trip to Lawton's camp within two hours of his arrival.

Soon thereafter Wood met with near tragedy in the form of a bite by a tarantula. At first he tried to ignore the swelling in his leg, but the symptoms worsened. At one stop, he spent a whole day in a cold stream attempting to reduce the fever he was suffering. At one point, Lawton feared that he would be forced to abandon his most trusted subordinate. Fortunately, at about that time Wood's fever broke. It was a close call.

The pursuit of Geronimo never penetrated Mexican territory more than two hundred miles from the United States border, but the total distance covered, back and forth, has been estimated at about thirteen hundred miles. At one point, Lawton's men overtook the Geronimo party and scattered them, taking most of their horses. Still the Indians always escaped. The Americans and Apache scouts were worn out, but so were Geronimo and his people.

Under those conditions, Miles risked the wrath of the president by changing tactics. He decided to use the carrot as well as the stick. He called on the services of Lieutenant Charles B. Gatewood, a thirty–three–year–old veteran of the Indian campaigns who, as a close associate of George Crook's, was trusted by Geronimo and could speak the Apache tongue. Miles sent Gatewood to join Lawton, with orders to find Geronimo and promise the Apache chief that, if he surrendered, he and his band would be spared any further violence. They would be sent to Florida, the instructions went on, but after two years would be allowed to return to the West. Gatewood, in bad health, disliked this assignment but had no choice but to carry it out.[5] When he reported to Lawton, he found that the captain liked the idea even less. Lawton, in fact, refused to participate in Miles's new approach.[6]

Gatewood, accompanied by Wood, made one unsuccessful effort to find Geronimo. Soon thereafter, however, Lawton's expedition overtook him at a place called the Baxispe River, near Douglas, Arizona. At that point, Gatewood

4. Ibid., 72.

5. Gatewood, still a lieutenant, died of stomach cancer in 1896.

6. A witness, James Parker, thought Lawton was secretly glad Gatewood had come. Ibid., 85.

assumed personal responsibility. Taking only two Apache scouts as escorts, he entered the Apache camp, where Geronimo greeted him with a warm embrace. They talked for three hours, apparently to no avail, and Gatewood returned to Lawton's camp certain that his mission had failed. The next day, to everyone's surprise, Geronimo actually sought Gatewood out. "If you will give me your word that we can meet General Miles with safety," he declared, "we will go to him and accept his terms, throwing ourselves on his mercy." Gatewood gave his word.[7] The date was August 24, 1886. The pursuit had gone on for nearly four months.[8]

The two groups—Geronimo's and Lawton's—traveled back to meet General Miles at Skeleton Valley. They went parallel, keeping some distance between them. There the surrender agreement was signed. On September 8, 1886, Geronimo and a pitiful little band of 134 people boarded a train bound for Florida. There they would be incarcerated for a couple of years pending repatriation to the West. But when their exile came to an end, they were sent to Oklahoma, not Arizona. The Indian Wars of the Southwest were at an end.

Wood had distinguished himself, proving himself indispensable to Lawton and the whole expedition. The regard Lawton held for him was illustrated by a letter he wrote his wife at a point where he feared that Wood might die: "I don't know what I would do if it was not for Dr. Wood. He is the best officer I ever had with me. If I had three or four, or rather if all my officers were like him, I would catch Geronimo in short order."[9]

There were also tangible rewards. First, Wood received an appointment as a first lieutenant in the Army Medical Corps, Regular Army. Second, he was nominated for the Medal of Honor. Although the decoration took years to process, Wood was no longer a mere contract surgeon. He was, in military circles at least, a hero of a dramatic expedition.

The capture of Geronimo was lavishly celebrated by the people of Arizona, who had lived in terror of that fierce warrior for more than twenty years. Liquor and oratory both flowed in the extended revelry, and some of the revelry lasted for as much as two weeks. Miles, Lawton, and Wood, in particular, were feted.[10]

The expedition at an end, Miles was reassigned to California. He attempted to keep Wood at his side for other assignments, but the request was denied. Unfortunately, both men had incurred the wrath of the authorities in

7. Ibid., 91–92.

8. See West Point, annual reunion of 1896, memorial article by Charles B. Gatewood.

9. Ibid., 85.

10. Unfortunately, the man most responsible for Geronimo's ultimate capitulation,

Washington. Cleveland was angry at Miles for his leniency in accepting the surrender of Geronimo. Wood, on his part, had earned his own share of enmity. In his official report as the senior physician at Huachuca, he listed the deficiencies in the uniforms the troops were required to wear, the quality of their shoes, and other matters. It was probably no coincidence, therefore, that Miles's routine request was disapproved. They did not lose contact, however. At Huachuca, Wood was free to travel, so when Miles broke his leg in Los Angeles, Wood was able to hurry to his side. Once there, he defied the judgment of a senior doctor that Miles's foot should be amputated. Wood saved Miles's foot—and the career of a future general in chief.

Returning to Huachuca, Wood was assigned a tactical mission, to lead a small detachment into the Sierra Madre in pursuit of a few Apache who had fled in preference to being sent to Florida. After two and a half months, Wood abandoned the chase, but the mission reinforced his extraordinary set of dual qualifications, as a doctor and as a line officer.

Eventually, Wood was transferred to San Francisco. There he met a young lady, Louise Condit Smith, an adopted "niece" of Stephen Field, a distinguished justice of the United States Supreme Court. Although Wood soon won the girl's affections, her adopted uncle thought the lady needed more time before engaging in marriage. He took her back to Washington with him, while Wood stayed in California. It would be 1890 before the lovers could regain contact in Washington. They were married in the justice's home on November 8 of that year.

Eventually, in 1894, Wood was assigned to Washington in his medical capacity to serve under the newly appointed Army surgeon General George Sternberg. The position of assistant attending surgeon was a prestigious spot, and at first Wood's appointment predictably ran into resistance from President Cleveland, who recalled Wood's accurate but nearly insubordinate report after the Geronimo campaign. Wood's cause was not aided by the fact that his two main backers, Miles and Field, were on the outs with Cleveland. Finally, however, the secretary of war, Daniel S. Lamont, approved Wood's appointment. He made it quite clear, however, that the appointment had been made strictly on the strength of Wood's military record, not because of his patronage. It was a triumph of meritocracy at its best.

In Washington Wood prospered, professionally and personally. Though officially assigned as the physician to all the Army officers on duty in the city, he also served as personal physician to President Cleveland, who discovered

---

Lieutenant Charles Gatewood, as a "George Crook man," was not included. Some jealousy of Gatewood's new fame may have been involved.

that he enjoyed taking the young doctor on hunting and fishing trips. In 1897 incoming president William McKinley kept him in this capacity. Although Wood was big and tough, he possessed a gentle manner, and he soon became the favorite of McKinley's ailing wife, who was also a confirmed hypochondriac. Leonard and Louise Wood were social favorites about town.

It was at that time that Captain Leonard Wood and Assistant Secretary of the Navy Theodore Roosevelt met, early in June 1897.

4

The Path to War

Roosevelt and Wood, having discovered how much they had in common, had no intention of allowing their new friendship to die. Because their places of work were so close—Wood's in the White House and Roosevelt's in the State–War–Navy Building across the street—getting together was easy. They developed a habit of taking long walks together in nearby Rock Creek Park whenever they could.[1] As both men craved physical exercise, they climbed ledges and went through various exercises on the way. They may have discussed many things, but one subject they emphasized most was that of Cuba.

The matter of American attitude toward Cuba—or, to be more exact, Spain—moved steadily toward the forefront. As they discussed this development, Roosevelt and Wood became more and more convinced that the United States should invade and free the Cubans from Spanish tyranny. The brutal measures being taken by the new Spanish viceroy, General Valeriano Weyler y Nicolau, were too harsh for the United States to stand by. Sober people might point out that the Spanish garrison in Cuba was strong and that the US Army, after many reductions since the Civil War, was in a state best described as its "dark ages." Despite all that, Roosevelt, Wood, and others believed the country should mobilize its strength to do whatever was necessary.

Wood's status as a captain in the Army placed inhibitions on him when it came to public speaking. Roosevelt, however, was a political appointee, and he was therefore afforded a great deal of leeway. His tendency to speak his mind was encouraged by the lassitude of his immediate boss, Secretary of the Navy John D. Long. In contrast to the dynamic Roosevelt, Long has been

1. Wood was not Roosevelt's only companion in Rock Creek Park. He also went there with Henry Cabot Lodge. With Lodge, however, the two rode horseback.

described as "small, soft, and plump." He possessed no naval background, and he showed little interest in learning much about his charge. His attitude toward the Navy was considered "laissez faire."[2] That attitude was just to Roosevelt's liking.

Despite Roosevelt's public statements urging war with Spain, his official position was limited to matters in that area, and only "as directed" by Long at that. And even if he had confined his activities to naval affairs, there would have been enough to occupy his mind, because the condition of the Navy could stand a great deal of improvement. It would have been worth his time and effort, because the Navy would be critical to the war he was promoting. Of this he was well aware. On June 2, 1887, shortly before his first meeting with Wood, Roosevelt had addressed the students of the Naval War College at Newport, citing George Washington's famous advice, "To be prepared for war is the most effectual means to promote peace." Not content to cite generalities, he made use of scare tactics, mentioning darkly that the Japanese were patrolling off the Hawaiian Islands with an armored cruiser. His fear, however, was mixed with a touch of admiration; he asserted that the Japanese possessed the martial spirit being lost by the Europeans. And then, carried away, he added, "No triumph of peace is quite so great as the supreme triumphs of war. . . . It may be that at some time in the dim future of the race the need for war will vanish, but that time is yet ages distant. As yet no nation can hold its place in the world, or can do any work really worth doing, unless it stands ready to guard its rights with an armed hand."[3]

As time went on, the United States drifted ever closer to war with Spain. It was a unilateral shifting of opinion; neither Spain nor the other European nations encouraged it. And nowhere was support for war greater than in the press. Two rival newspapers, William Randolph Hearst's *New York Journal* and Joseph Pulitzer's *New York World,* both in financial trouble and needing a war to increase circulation, continued to supply sensational headlines in a writing style that came to be called "yellow journalism." Of the two, Hearst, who had once worked for Pulitzer, was the younger and more zealous in promoting the war in Cuba, but Pulitzer was not to be discounted. Both papers blazoned on their front pages stories of atrocities perpetrated by the Spanish in Cuba.

Hearst was unusually aggressive and able to persuade reporters of reputation to go to Havana. Among them were Stephen Crane, a newspaperman

2. Edmund Morris, *The Rise of Theodore Roosevelt,* 566.
3. Ibid., 359.

immortalized by his book *The Red Badge of Courage*, and veteran war correspondent Richard Harding Davis. Frederic Remington provided Hearst with sketches. To Remington, who was bored and wanted to return home, Hearst was reputed to have said, "You furnish the sketches and I'll furnish the war." Weyler, strangely, granted permission for these three to roam at various times through the Cuban territory. The reality of what they saw was bad enough: confinement and starvation in restless areas. But the stories lost nothing in the telling. Many of the reports were downright falsehoods, and they succeeded in creating mania in the American public.

Despite the growing pressures, President McKinley refused to panic. He kept steady diplomatic pressure on the Spanish government and was successful. The success, however, only brought matters to a head in Cuba. Weyler was recalled from Havana, and the Spanish government promised the Cuban people more autonomy under Spanish rule. But enough of the Spanish population was favorable to autocratic rule that riots broke out in the streets, riots so severe that the American consul general in Havana, Fitzhugh Lee, asked for a major naval vessel to be sent to safeguard the American citizens. McKinley held off at first. He brushed off such incidents as the interception of a letter written by the Spanish minister in Washington, José Canalejas, criticizing the Americans and calling McKinley himself "weak" and "a bidder for the admiration of the crowd."[4] McKinley, however, had been a major in the Civil War, a veteran of Antietam and other bloody battles, and he knew from personal experience what war was about. He did not want to see another one.

Nevertheless, the tensions still continued to worsen. In January 1898, McKinley began to take Fitzhugh Lee's requests for naval protection more seriously. In this he was probably influenced by Lee's unusual stature. Not only was he the nephew of Confederate general Robert E. Lee, but in his own right he had been commander of the Confederate cavalry at Appomattox. Furthermore, Lee had been one of the earliest advocates of reconciliation between North and South after the end of the war. He had served as governor of Virginia (1886–90) and had been a strong supporter of Grover Cleveland in the presidential campaign of 1892. When McKinley took office in 1897, he had kept Fitzhugh Lee in his present position as "a man of integrity and judgment." Lee's post as consul general was largely a facade; his main responsibility was to function as an adviser on both diplomatic and military matters—"our man in Havana."

4. Dale L. Walker, *The Boys of '98: Theodore Roosevelt and the Rough Riders*, 53.

McKinley finally took action. He dispatched the battleship *Maine* to Havana. It was a logical ship to send; despite its designation as a "battleship," it was only a sixty–six–hundred–ton "predreadnaught" vessel, currently employed in coastal patrolling. Its presence in Havana could be viewed by the Spanish as somewhat routine.

The Spanish accepted the visit of the *Maine* as the friendly gesture it was purported to be—or at least pretended to. The *Maine* and the Spanish warship the *Alfonso XII* exchanged proper salutes, and the captain of the *Maine,* Charles D. Sigsbee, made the proper protocol calls into Havana. The formalities were only on the surface, however. Sigsbee was disturbed to see so many signs with "Viva Weyler" and "Death to the United States" blazoned on them, and someone even slipped a note into his hand expressing the same sentiments. But there was nothing for him to do but sit out his time moored in Havana Harbor. A highlight of the stay was a visit to the *Maine* by the seventy–four–year–old Clara Barton, president of the American Red Cross. She had come to view conditions in the city to see what if anything the Red Cross should offer by way of assistance to the Cuban population.

On the evening of February 15, 1898, disaster struck. At 9:40, Captain Sigsbee, in his cabin, felt a violent explosion belowdecks, caused by the detonation of an estimated five tons of gunpowder below the forward guns, unfortunately the area in which men were sleeping. The losses were heavy: 274 men dead and only 89 survivors. Most of the survivors, incidentally, were officers, whose sleeping quarters were located in a different part of the ship. An American ship in the harbor and the *Alfonso XII* did their best to rescue as many men as possible. Clara Barton, in the city, set up a hospital facility to care for the wounded.

The cause of the disaster was not determined to everyone's satisfaction—and it is not absolutely certain to this day—but the Americans, especially the yellow press, lost no time in declaring that the *Maine* had been sunk by a Spanish mine floating in the harbor. A naval court of inquiry headed by Rear Admiral William T. Sampson decided as much by March 21, 1898, and its conclusions were supported, if a bit tentatively, by Sigsbee himself. Although the bulk of subsequent investigations pointed to spontaneous combustion in the coal, that possibility was discounted at the time.

Roosevelt and Wood now saw war as imminent, and Wood's elation apparently showed. On the morning after the news came in, President McKinley half in jest directed a question to him: "Captain Wood, have you and Theodore Roosevelt declared war yet?" "No sir," Wood answered, "but we think you will."

McKinley, however, was still not convinced of the need for war. Always thinking back to his own experience during the Civil War, he was heard to declare, "I shall never get in a war until I am sure that God and man approve. I have been through one war; I have seen the dead piled up, and I do not want to see another."[5] He was not alone in his thinking.

Secretary of the Navy Long also refused to view the sinking of the *Maine* as a cause for war. He did not muzzle Roosevelt when the latter expressed his warlike views, but he was confident that his impetuous subordinate could take no official action. So Roosevelt had to be somewhat subtle in the actions he did take. However, he did significant things. One involved the Asiatic Fleet. In conjunction with Senator Lodge, Roosevelt had arranged for Commodore George Dewey, who shared Roosevelt's aggressive views, to be assigned to that command. Roosevelt could be sure that the ambitious Dewey would be looking for action. In public Roosevelt played a promotional game, making it a point to praise Secretary Long lavishly, biding his time.

Finally, on Saturday, February 25, 1898, ten days after the *Maine* disaster, Roosevelt saw a chance to take far–reaching action. The secretary decided to make a visit to New England, leaving Roosevelt in charge of the department. Roosevelt, his plans laid, sent an order to Dewey in Hong Kong: "Order the squadron, except the *Monocacy*, to Hong Kong. Keep full of coal. In the event of war [with] Spain, your duty will be to see that the Spanish squadron does not leave the Asiatic coast, and then offensive operations in [the] Philippine Islands."[6]

Roosevelt had stuck his neck way out, but Long, on his return to Washington, did not seem perturbed. In any event, he did not reverse Roosevelt's action. (Perhaps Roosevelt had done what Long had not dared to do.) As events turned out, Long would later have cause to be grateful.

Somewhat as a sidelight, Roosevelt was amused to note the change on the part of many former pacifists, once opponents of preparedness, who were now in a state of panic, expecting Spanish ships to appear off the coast at any moment. In his autobiography, he cites an incident he considered typical. A senator from a seaboard state had previously opposed building up the Navy. "But now," according to Roosevelt, "[he] demanded that a ship be anchored in the harbor of [the] city as Protection." Receiving no satisfaction from the Navy Department, the senator began hectoring President McKinley. The president, who very much needed his support, finally ordered the Navy

5. Hagedorn, *Leonard Wood, a Biography,* 1:141.
6. Roosevelt, *An Autobiography,* 214.

to comply. Roosevelt did so. The ship he sent, however, was a leftover monitor from the Civil War with one smooth gun, crewed by a score of naval militia. Despite the risk, the ship was able to navigate the trip, and the solon's constituents were satisfied. In fact, as Roosevelt put it, "the ship would not have been a formidable foe to any antagonists . . . than those of Alcibiades."[7]

Despite his responsibilities in the Navy Department, Roosevelt had no intention of sitting out the war behind a desk, especially as he had played such a role in swinging public opinion in its favor. Perhaps partially influenced by memories of his adored father's avoiding service in the Civil War, he determined to serve in the front ranks himself. He recognized his lack of technical expertise in military matters, but he believed that his experience in the Dakotas qualified him as a cavalryman. He therefore confronted the secretary of war, Russell A. Alger, with the idea of raising a volunteer cavalry regiment.

Alger was sympathetic to Roosevelt's proposal, but as a veteran of the Civil War himself, he thought it misplaced. The idea of anyone's stepping down from a subcabinet position to that of a regimental officer did not make sense to him. Alger further looked askance at Roosevelt's request that the colonel in command of the regiment should be Leonard Wood, a mere captain in the Medical Corps. But in Roosevelt's rather ponderous account:

> I told him that after six weeks' service in the field I would feel competent to handle the regiment, but that I would not know how to equip it or how to get it into the first action, but that Wood was entirely competent at once to take command, and that if he would make Wood colonel I would accept the lieutenant–colonelcy. . . . I did not wish to ride on any man's shoulders; that I hoped to be given every chance that my deeds and abilities warranted; but that I did not wish what I did not earn.

Alger gave in. He authorized the creation of the 1st United States Voluntary Cavalry Regiment with Leonard Wood in command and Theodore Roosevelt as the lieutenant colonel. Because the regiment would be recruited from the southwestern part of the country, it soon came to be known as the Rough Riders.[8]

Roosevelt sensibly remained at his post as assistant secretary of the Navy while the details of making these arrangements were being worked out. He planned to stay in his position until war should actually be declared. He had

7. Ibid., 216–17.
8. Ibid., 218.

no intention of resigning his prestigious place in the hierarchy without the prospect of fighting. The odds of war, however, were overwhelming. The American people were now becoming bent on freeing Cuba from Spanish rule, and Spain had no intention of giving up its last remaining possession in the West Indies, at least not without a fight. As time went on, even President McKinley was beginning to believe that war was justified.

In the days before radio communications, not everyone was aware of the growing tensions. On February 18, the Spanish cruiser *Vizcaya,* completely unaware of recent events, sailed into New York Harbor, expecting to be welcomed as a return courtesy call in exchange for the visit of the *Maine* to Havana. For some reason, the *Vizcaya* stayed in port for a few days, though the atmosphere must have been cool. It then sailed for Havana.

By now the Spanish government had had enough of Fitzhugh Lee and requested that the consul general be recalled. Lee was only too happy to leave, but he would go only after he had made certain that all American citizens willing to depart should be removed. Two days later, on March 8, Congress authorized an appropriation of fifty million dollars for a war fund.

The drift to war continued to move inexorably. On March 26, 1898, President McKinley received the Sampson report, which concluded that the *Maine* had been destroyed by a floating Spanish mine. Ignoring the findings of a similar study done by Spanish authorities that found the explosion to have been an internal affair, McKinley sent the report with at least an implied endorsement to Congress.

By March 30, the war had really started. On that day, the American minister in Madrid confronted the Spanish government, demanding that Spain cease hostilities against the insurgents in Cuba and grant the island independence. The Spanish throne angrily rejected the demand the next day. On receipt of the refusal, the US Congress authorized an appropriation of twenty–two million dollars for naval construction.

The American bellicosity was not popular elsewhere around the world. Pope Leo XIII, who felt a proprietary interest in the welfare of any Catholic country, called on President McKinley to restrain from war, pending current negotiations. In Washington the ambassadors of five countries—England, France, Germany, Italy, and Russia—seconded the pope's request. The Spanish themselves did their best to avert the conflict, directing General Ramón Blanco y Erenas, their representative in Cuba, to declare a truce with the Cuban insurrectionists. On that same day, Fitzhugh Lee left Havana.

The debate in Congress over a declaration of war with Spain created far more heat than it produced light. It was complicated by dissension within the Republican ranks, although the issue was not being argued along strictly party lines. The Speaker of the House of Representatives, "Czar" Tom Reed, was a Republican, a good friend of Lodge and Roosevelt, but he split with them in that he was determined to avoid war with Spain. As long ago as three years before, in fact, Reed had blocked a move among House Republicans to recognize the Cuban insurgents formally as belligerents, much to the displeasure of Hearst's *Journal*.

But in the spring of 1898, the enthusiasm for war was steadily growing, and Reed's once unchallengeable power was waning. Still, he was ready to sacrifice his position for principle. Tom Reed stuck to his guns.

In view of the worsening relations between the United States and Spain, President McKinley finally decided, on April 11, to send a message to Congress, requesting the right of armed intervention in Cuba. He intended to put pressure on Spain to free Cuba, but his seven–thousand–word message stopped short of asking for a declaration of war, as Roosevelt and other war advocates had hoped. The Republican disappointment did not result in drastic action, however. Loyal party men such as Senator Lodge supported the president, much to Roosevelt's unhappiness.

The debate is remembered not for the rhetoric but for its violence. Two days after McKinley's message reached the floor of Congress, somebody, in a state of passion, hit someone who held opposing views, and before long a melee was in progress. Shouts of "Liar!" and "Scoundrel!" rang through the halls. Arms flailed. It was, however, a nearly bloodless riot—the only casualty was a page boy knocked temporarily unconscious by a blow to the jaw. But the lack of dignity was huge, causing the *Times* of London to offer this sardonic quip: "Such is the body in whose favour the President on Monday abdicated his rightful authority and to whom he entrusted the fortunes of his and their country."[9] The *Times* may have been ignorant of the American constitutional provision that grants Congress the right to declare war, but the episode did nothing to enhance American prestige abroad.

The matter was finally settled, not by the US Congress but by the Spanish themselves. Whether the Americans realized it or not, the country's policies and attitudes had generated rage against America among the people of Spain themselves. On the early morning of April 21, therefore, the Spanish foreign minister in Madrid informed the American ambassador that Spain had broken relations with the United States. The same morning, the United States Atlantic Fleet slipped out of the harbor at Norfolk, bound for the Caribbe-

9. Evan Thomas, *The War Lovers*, 247.

an. Two days later, President McKinley called for an expansion of the Regular Army to twenty–eight thousand men, and a million men volunteered for service.[10]

Congress took its time to debate the issue. During the debate discussions, Senator Henry M. Teller, of Colorado, inserted an amendment to the draft resolution, stating categorically that the United States had no intention of annexing Cuba as an American possession. It was an important provision. In addition to placing the US government on a high moral plane, it ensured that the Cuban insurrectionists, led by General Calixto Garcia, would fight on the American side. On April 19, the US Congress declared Cuba to be independent, and four days later, on April 23, Spain declared war on the United States. Congress reciprocated by a declaration on April 25, with President McKinley making the action retroactive to April 22. The United States must make the first move.

The die was now cast. In Hong Kong, Commodore George Dewey, prepared for action by the order of Theodore Roosevelt back in February, amassed his eight ships and headed for Manila. Steaming through the passage of Manila Bay past Corregidor and past Cavite, he destroyed the pitiful, hapless six gunboats of Spanish admiral Patricio Montojo. Dewey's "victory" was achieved without the loss of a single man.

The war was on. Theodore Roosevelt, his work in the Navy Department finished, resigned his position as assistant secretary and assumed his duties as the lieutenant colonel of the 1st United States Voluntary Cavalry Regiment.

10. Ibid., 243.

5

On to Cuba

Leonard Wood knew that his appointment as a line officer, even of volunteers, would cause resentment in the Regular Army. However, his ambition far overcame his inhibitions. He knew he was prepared for that transition, for in his off hours throughout his years of doctoring he had been studying tactics and military history with a view to this end. On learning of the sinking of the *Maine,* therefore, he had lost no time in approaching President McKinley and volunteering his services as a line officer of any grade. McKinley refused the request, primarily because he hated to lose the services of the doctor upon whom his sick wife was so dependent. The president, however, promised not to stand in Wood's way if he could attain his goals by dealing directly with the Army authorities.

Wood's task in convincing the Army authorities was more difficult than manipulating McKinley, for the regulars, especially the West Pointers, believed they had a monopoly on military knowledge. Wood's recent award of the Medal of Honor, which had been pending for a dozen years, did little to further his cause, because his services in earning it had involved duties other than those of a line officer.

Unable to sell himself to the War Department, Wood resolved to attain his ends as a volunteer, the appointee of a state governor. Armed with lavish recommendations from Roosevelt, Army chief Nelson Miles, and even Secretary of War Alger, he approached the governor of his home state of Massachusetts. The governor, however, had no intention of organizing such a regiment. Wood also met failure in New York, but for another reason: that governor had his own favorite son in case such a unit should be called up.

Finally, fortune smiled from two directions. Roosevelt had begun his campaign, and the governor of Arizona, where Wood was still a big hero, decided to contribute a volunteer unit as a gift to the nation. Senator Francis Warren of Wyoming was also creating a similar unit. Secretary Alger finally agreed to organize several volunteer regiments, of which three would be cavalry. The first would be commanded by Wood, with Roosevelt as his lieutenant colonel. It was really a political act; the professional head of the Army, General Miles, appeared to lack interest in organizing any volunteer regiments at all.[1]

But Roosevelt had broken the bureaucratic barriers, and Wood's greatest ambitions had been exceeded: he was to be the colonel of a regiment. He was ready. Once his appointment had been confirmed, he flew into action. He even knew the location where he wanted the regiment to be recruited and trained: a large piece of unoccupied territory near San Antonio, Texas. He also knew what he wanted in other matters. He insisted, for example, on issuing his troopers a lightweight tan uniform, far different from the heavy blue of the regulars. He also knew the type of boots he wanted, based on the report he had sent to Washington from Arizona many years previously. In the matter of armament, he would accept only the best. He demanded that his men be issued the same rifles as those of the regulars, the new Krag–Jørgensen. Wood made all these arrangements informally with the chief of ordnance and the quartermaster general, but to implement them officially he needed to have them ordered formally by the secretary of war. Taking no chances on Alger's shilly–shallying, Wood brought the stack of orders for his requests into the secretary's office all at once. In a short period, a bewildered Alger had given Wood all that he wanted. Wood was then ready to depart Washington for San Antonio.

On arriving at his destination, Wood had many urgent tasks to accomplish. Although there would be overlap, he had a set of priorities. First was sanitation, second was housing, third was the reception of incoming packets of troops, then came the issue of clothing and equipment, and finally came the instruction of noncommissioned officers. Mixed with all these activities were training of new recruits, care of mounts, drill, and ceremonies. Wood performed this program with quiet dignity and intensity.

Occasionally, Wood slipped out of his role. On one occasion, when a young soldier was flung against a tree by a recalcitrant mount, the colonel was quickly on his knees beside him: the commanding officer had temporarily been

1. In the chapter above, note that one reason Roosevelt wanted Wood to command the regiment was speed. He foresaw a short war, and he was afraid that his own inexperience in Army bureaucracy would cause such delay that the Rough Riders might not get off to Cuba in time for the fighting. This was exactly what happened to the other two volunteer regiments.

transformed into a physician. He took pride in the regiment and his role as its commanding officer. It was always, despite public perception, Wood's regiment.

Although Roosevelt's appointment as Wood's lieutenant colonel was effective in early–May 1898, he did not leave Washington for Texas immediately. He and Wood had decided that he would be more useful for the moment by staying behind to see to it that the War Department came through with its promises—even written orders. It was well that Roosevelt did so, because the administrative services were slow to respond. On May 10, however, Roosevelt was able to send a message to the friend he now called "Colonel Wood": "I spent a good deal of yesterday and today fussing with the Ordnance and Quartermaster General's Department. They have sent out tracers and tell me that by day after tomorrow the rifles and most of the supplies will be at San Antonio. I hope you got your horses pretty well purchased by this time. The enclosed letter shows that you are allowed to purchase over the number if necessary."[2]

Roosevelt had another incentive to stay in the East for a while. He was resolved to do some recruiting among men he particularly wanted. He made visits to the campuses of Ivy League universities, especially his own alma mater, Harvard. His theme, which seems startling today, was that the privileged classes of American society must take the lead in fighting the war. So effective were his efforts that he found himself somewhat embarrassed by the fact that he was overwhelmed with men intent on joining him. He finally selected about fifty, among them two star football quarterbacks from Harvard, a champion high jumper, a former US tennis champion, and a group of polo players. He did not, however, restrict himself to the universities; he also signed up some former members of the New York Police Force. He took great pride in the fact that almost none of these volunteers asked to come in as commissioned officers; they were content to serve as privates.[3]

The easterners whom Roosevelt had recruited would actually constitute only a small fraction of the twelve hundred men of the Rough Riders, but Roosevelt's visibility in recruiting them gave the public the impression that the regiment was Roosevelt's. At one point, a friend of Wood's from New York wrote in protest. "The newspapers about here keep talking about Roosevelt's regiment. Give the reporters a bit of discipline and have things called by their right name."[4] This type of thing did not make Wood happy, but he took it

2. H. W. Brands, ed., *The Selected Letters of Theodore Roosevelt,* 181.
3. Theodore Roosevelt, *The Rough Riders,* 14–15.
4. Hagedorn, *Leonard Wood, a Biography,* 1:151.

philosophically. Not long after, Wood wrote a friend: "It was not long after I had been joined by Roosevelt at San Antonio, when I realized that if the campaign lasted for any considerable length of time I would be kicked upstairs to make room for the promotion of Roosevelt. I decided that, if that should happen, I would see to it that no matter in what situation I found myself, I would find justification of my being there and find a job that needed doing and would do it with all my power."[5]

Despite the publicity engendered by Roosevelt's activities in the East, the basic character of the regiment followed the style of rough men from the Southwest. Most were cowboys and ranchers, although the roster also included professional men. To take them in, Wood had asked the local governors to set up about a dozen reception centers. Once his men were inducted and sworn in, they were subjected to extensive training, so intensive that the 1st United States Volunteer Cavalry Regiment became known as the "Rough Riders," the name that has lived on in history.

Roosevelt, despite his time in the Dakotas, was highly impressed by the sturdiness of the men of the regiment. In a letter to Senator Lodge, he bubbled with enthusiasm:

> It is as typical an American regiment as ever marched or fought. I suppose that about 95 per cent of the men are of native birth, but we have a few from everywhere, including a score of Indians and about as many men of Mexican origin from New Mexico, then there are some fifty Easterners—almost all graduates of Harvard, Yale, Princeton, etc,—and almost as many southerners, the rest are from the plains and the Rocky Mountains. Three fourths of our men have at one time or another been cowboys or small stockmen, certainly two thirds have fathers who fought on one side or the other in the civil war. . . . These men are in [the Army] because they want to be in it. They are intelligent as well as game.[6]

Roosevelt was also content with the quality of his officers. Many of them were veterans of the Regular Army, who had fought against Apache, Ute, and Cheyenne. Some had previously been federal marshals. One individual whom Roosevelt singled out for praise was Bucky O'Neill, the current mayor of Prescott, Arizona. O'Neill had taken a leave of absence from civic duties to command Troop "A." Roosevelt described him as "a famous sheriff

5. Ibid., 157.
6. Brands, *T. R.*, 341.

throughout the West for his feats of victorious warfare against the Apache, no less than against the white road–agents and man–killers. His father had fought in Meagher's Brigade[7] in the Civil War, and he himself was a born soldier, a born leader of men. He was a wild, reckless fellow, soft spoken, and of dauntless courage and boundless ambition; he was staunchly loyal to his friends, and cared for them in every way."[8]

Roosevelt even evaluated himself. "I have been both astonished and pleased," he wrote to Lodge, "at my own ability in the line of tactics. I thoroughly enjoy handling these men, and I get them on the jump so that they execute their movements at a gallop."[9]

Roosevelt had harbored one concern in gathering such a group of individuals. How would they tolerate the discipline that the Army would necessarily impose on them? In this matter, however, he described himself as "agreeably disappointed." By and large, the men realized the difference between an army and a mob. But to keep them in such a frame of mind, the leaders—meaning himself—had to be strong. He and Wood quietly but firmly corrected infractions of protocol that would seem trivial in the more relaxed Army of later years. For example, a man would be corrected if he said, "Good evening, sir," when saluting the colonel. The salute was sufficient in itself. On one occasion, a mess sergeant, in calling dinner, was corrected for referring to the officers as "you fellers." All these small admonitions were taken in good part.[10]

But Roosevelt himself still had to absorb some of the ways of the military hierarchy. One incident, which he chose not to describe to Lodge in his letters, involved his natural generosity, exuberance, and love of applause. One day, after finishing a drill with one of his units, he ordered the men to dismount and then shouted, "The men can go in and drink all the beer they want, which I will pay for." This gesture elicited such a response that Roosevelt got carried away. He joined them for a couple of hours.

Nearly everyone in the camp thought well of Roosevelt's boyish enthusiasm, but one who did not was Leonard Wood. That evening Wood sent for his lieutenant colonel and pointed out that, in the interests of discipline, officers did not drink with enlisted men. Roosevelt accepted the chiding seriously and left Wood's tent. In a few seconds, however, his embarrassment overcame him. He returned to the tent, stood rigidly at attention, saluted, and made a

7. The famous Irish Brigade from New York.
8. Roosevelt, *The Rough Riders,* 19–20.
9. Brands, *T. R.,* 342.
10. Roosevelt, *The Rough Riders,* 32–33.

stiff speech that ended, "Sir, I consider myself the damndest ass within ten miles of this camp! Good night, sir!"[11]

Roosevelt's enthusiasm for his military activities was admirable for a soldier, but in broader matters it beclouded his judgment. His obsession to see battle with the Rough Riders, for example, caused him to forget that the purpose of an army is to enforce the national will. In one letter, he exhorted Senator Lodge to do everything possible to prevent any successful negotiations between Washington and Madrid, even if such negotiations would grant the Americans everything—the Philippines, Puerto Rico, Guam, and even Cuba—without a fight.[12] He, Roosevelt, must defeat the Spanish in battle for the sake of the battle itself.

As is always the case when a unit prepares to break camp, Wood was involved in so many administrative matters that he was forced to turn over much of the training to Roosevelt, who relished the activity. He began by drilling the men on foot, which in itself is difficult enough. Then, when he was satisfied with his men's precision, he began practicing maneuvers on horseback. The fact that many of the horses were not broken in caused very little problem; many of the Rough Riders were sufficiently strong and adept that no horse could remain unbroken. As for weapons, Wood had decided to rely on only the Krag carbine, which he had successfully obtained, and the revolver. To the disapproval of more formal Regular Army cavalry officers, the Rough Riders dispensed with the saber. They were, after all, expecting to do a great deal of their fighting on foot, with their mounts being held by horse holders in the rear.[13]

11. Brands, *T. R.*, 342. Roosevelt's speech was actually a little longer. As Wood reported it, with some amusement, he was extremely formal: "I want to talk with you, sir. I listened to what you said this afternoon. You are quite right, quite proper. I wish to tell you, sir, that I took the squadron, without thinking of the question of the officers drinking with their men, and gave them all a schooner of beer. I wish to say, sir, that I agree with what you said. I consider myself the damndest ass within ten miles of this camp. Goodnight." And off he went. Hagedorn, *Leonard Wood, a Biography*, 1:154.

12. American annexation of Cuba on a permanent basis was not at issue. The declaration of war on April 20, 1898, disclaimed "any intention to exercise sovereignty, jurisdiction, or control of the island or its people." Quoted in Morris, *Rise of Theodore Roosevelt*, 613.

13. European cavalrymen have contended that American cavalry is misnamed; US mounted warriors have always been what they termed dragoons. There is something to be said for that, but there is a reason. Due to the density of the country's underbrush and hillocks, even the plains of America have rarely provided the broad fields for cavalry sweeps that the fields of Europe provided.

Although Wood and Roosevelt had trained hard during the month of May 1898, they were still uncertain whether they would ever be employed in actual fighting. Their worries dissipated, however, at the end of the month, when a cablegram arrived at San Antonio, ordering the regiment to leave by train for Tampa, Florida, to join a force being assembled, presumably for an invasion of Cuba. Wood, on receiving the message, showed no emotion; he simply stood up, shook Roosevelt by the hand, and disclosed its contents. Roosevelt showed no such restraint; he whooped and hollered, and in no time the entire camp had the news. As the scene was described, "hats, blankets, tin cups, even saddles, skyward and made a bedlam of Colonel Wood's decorous camp of subjugated wild men."[14]

They had every cause to be proud. Among all the units scheduled for inclusion in the expedition, the Rough Riders were the only volunteer regiment. The other two volunteer cavalry regiments were not yet ready to go. The personality and influence of Theodore Roosevelt may also have been a factor in its selection—one suspects that it may have been critical.

On Sunday, May 29, the first three of seven sections, under the direct command of Wood, left the camp at San Antonio for the railroad station. With all the confusion, including the failure of trains to show up, Wood's contingent was forced to wait until midnight before pulling out. Roosevelt, in charge of the other four sections, arrived at the station about the time that Wood left; they were off by the next morning. Once under way, the sections spaced out. When one section stopped to allow the troopers to water and feed their horses, it would be the only one at that station.

Eventually, both officers and men were exhausted from the heat and lack of sleep. As usual the quartermaster seldom delivered enough water and forage to any one station. Wood therefore faced a continual battle. According to a letter he wrote home, he was forced to take "armed possession" of one train not assigned to him, though he did not specify details. Still, there were bright aspects. All along the line, people were aware that the famed Rough Riders were coming through and were out beside the tracks to greet them. In New Orleans, the crowds were particularly enthusiastic, and the sight of the American flag on proud display gave Wood a lift to realize that the hurts of the Civil War thirty years previously had been largely healed.[15]

After four grueling days of travel, the 1st United States Volunteer Cavalry Regiment reached Tampa at midnight on June 3, only to find the camp in a state

14. Hagedorn, *Leonard Wood, a Biography,* 155.
15. Ibid.; Roosevelt, *The Rough Riders,* 48.

of confusion. Veterans of the campaign later recalled their arrival as one of the blackest moments in the history of the US Army. According to Roosevelt:

> Tampa lay in the pine–covered sand–flats at the end of a one–track railroad, and everything connected with both military and railroad matters was in an almost inextricable tangle. There was no one to meet us or to tell us where we were to camp, and no one to issue us food for the first twenty–four hours; while the railroad people unloaded us wherever they pleased. . . . We had to buy the men food out of our own pockets, and to seize wagons in order to get our spare luggage taken to the camping ground which we at last found had been allotted to us.[16]

Soon, however, Wood established a semblance of order. The area was soon cleaned up, and drill had been instituted immediately. Wood arranged the camp in the standard manner: a rectangle with the twelve troops lined along the long sides with the officers' tents located at one end of the rectangle and the mess tents at the other. Everyone, especially the officers, worked hard and took no time for leisure, even though the town of Tampa was full of generals, members of the press, and fine ladies. Their industry was noticed, however, and attachés of various countries—English, German, Russian, French, and even Japanese—came out to visit them. Chapel services were held on the one Sunday the Rough Riders were at Tampa. The regiment was outstanding, even among the regulars.

The force being assembled was the United States Fifth Army Corps, commanded by Major General William R. Shafter, a sixty–three–year–old veteran of the Civil War and of numerous campaigns against the western Indians. Like Miles and Lawton, both of whom were friends, Shafter had been decorated with the Medal of Honor, in his case for action in the Civil War at Seven Pines in McClellan's Peninsular Campaign, in 1862. He had fought the Apache, and in the last gasp of the Indian Wars he had assisted Miles in dictating the final treaty with the Sioux after the Battle of Wounded Knee in 1890. He was known as sensible, if not brilliant, sometimes abrasive, but a man with a highly creditable record. Above all, he carried the rank of major general, befitting the command of a campaign of this importance.

Shafter's greatest drawback was his health. He was grossly overweight—three hundred pounds—and he reportedly suffered from gout. Nobody could

16. Ibid., 54–55.

expect him to conduct operations in the field on foot. But Miles had been able to convince Secretary Alger of Shafter's fitness for command, and he had been selected. The result in anticipated operations would inevitably be much delegation of authority on Shafter's part when the corps went into battle. But that would come out later.

Fortunately for Shafter's Fifth Corps, the stay at Tampa lasted only five days. When the time for departure approached, however, Wood and his men were in for another shock: the men's horses had to be left behind when the expedition sailed. Only the officers could be mounted. Worse, only eight of the twelve troops of the regiment could be included; four troops would have to be left behind. It was no easy task for Wood and Roosevelt to select which units should go. Wood was accorded some flexibility in individual cases, but not much. He managed, for example, to include Hamilton Fish, a great football star whom Roosevelt had recruited personally. Aware of Fish's qualities and desire to go, Captain Allyn Capron, commanding "K" Troop, had agreed to make an exception. Fish, as a sergeant, happily joined Capron in the coming adventure.[17]

Departure, however, was not to be easier than anything else at Tampa. On the evening of June 7, Wood received the order to move his eight troops to Post Tampa, nine miles away, to arrive by the next morning. The regiment, now down to about 560 men, appeared at the railroad siding in good order at midnight, where they were supposed to be loaded up and transported to their debarkation point. No train, however, showed up. At 3:00 a.m., Wood moved his men to another railhead, where again there was no train. According to Roosevelt's account, a couple of generals were witnessing from the sidelines, but none of them knew anything. At 6:00 a.m., some coal cars appeared, and Wood seized them and used them for transport. Finally, the regiment arrived at Port Tampa, the men covered with coal dust but in possession of all their belongings.

Once delivered to the pier, Wood and Roosevelt set out to find a ship to carry them. Ignoring another group of general officers (also lacking in information), they tracked down the depot quartermaster, who advised them that they would be assigned to the steamer *Yucatan,* which was about to make its way into the harbor. The *Yucatan* docked at the end of the pier, away from

17. Allyn Capron Jr. was the son of another Captain Allyn Capron, a West Point graduate in the class of 1867. The younger Capron was a regular officer, a second lieutenant in the 7th Cavalry. He had managed to secure a captaincy in the 1st Volunteer Cavalry, probably with the help of Roosevelt.

the point where the Rough Riders had been dropped, but Wood, with a few men, took possession of it. From its captain, he learned that two other regiments, the 2d Infantry and the 71st New York Volunteers, had also been allotted to the *Yucatan,* but the Rough Riders had possession, and their inclusion in Shafter's force was ensured.

Once on board, however, Shafter's expedition was again held up. A report had just come in that Spanish ships were sighted in the area. It took a week to ascertain that the ships someone had sighted were the transports destined for Tampa to transport Shafter's force. In the meantime, Wood and Roosevelt continued a training program aboard the *Yucatan.* Morale remained good despite intense heat and miserable rations.[18] On June 14, 1898, Shafter's Fifth Corps sailed out of Tampa Bay, bound for some unknown destination in Cuba. Just being under way lifted spirits.

On April 30, 1898, five days after the United States had declared war, Spanish admiral Pascual Cervera, with a flotilla of four armored cruisers and two torpedo boats, set sail from Cape Verde, bound for the Caribbean. This was no small venture; the fifty–nine–year–old Cervera was the foremost admiral of the Spanish navy, and his fleet, though recognized as inferior to that of the United States, was still a respectable one for the time. The *Pluton, Terror,* and *Puror* were among the best torpedo–armed warships in the world.

Cervera was desperately unhappy with the decision of the Spanish government to send him on this mission. Some of his ships were so much in need of repair that they could not function. The strategy he had been pleading with the authorities to adopt was to meet the Americans at the Canary Islands, assuming that they would attempt to invade the Spanish homeland. In his own backyard, Cervera would be close to his coaling stations, while the Americans would depend on a long supply line across the Atlantic. He later wrote of his consternation: "It is impossible for me to give you an idea of the surprise and consternation by all on the receipt of the order to sail. Indeed, that surprise is well justified, for nothing can be expected of this expedition except the total destruction of the fleet or its hasty and demoralized return." Nevertheless, Cervera was a dedicated professional seaman, so once he had exhausted his protests, he set sail with a heavy heart.

Cervera's operational orders were vague, because the situation in the Atlantic was so uncertain. One option open to him was to reinforce the Spanish fleet in Havana. Another, amazingly, was to sail to the Philippines. The

18. The abominable quality of a type of unsalted meat called "canned fresh beef."

mission he selected, however, was that advocated by his principal subordinate, Admiral Fernando Villaamil, to scatter his fleet along the American East Coast and terrorize the inhabitants. The policy was remarkably successful for a while. Panic struck the people in the region when they learned that an unknown number of Spanish ships were prowling offshore.

Finally, however, Cervera decided to concentrate his ships, if for no other purpose than to take on coal. The danger of encountering the superior American fleet ruled out his trying to reach Havana. Rejecting San Juan, Puerto Rico, he tried to obtain coal at Curaçao, Dutch West Indies, but found that the expected resupply from Spain had not appeared. Finally, in desperation, he sailed to the Bay of Santiago, on the eastern end on the south coast of Cuba. To the best of Cervera's knowledge, Santiago was the only Cuban port not yet blockaded by the Americans. By May 29, the day that Wood received orders to leave San Antonio for Tampa, Cervera's fleet, now grown to seven ships, was already in Santiago Harbor.[19]

Cervera's antagonist in this cat–and–mouse game, Admiral William T. Sampson, was as distinguished a seaman as Cervera himself. A member of the class of 1861 at the Naval Academy, he had commanded a ship at Charleston Harbor during the Civil War. He had served two tours as the superintendent of the Naval Academy. Most recently, before his promotion to rear admiral, he had headed the so–called Sampson Board, which ruled that the *Maine* had been destroyed by a Spanish mine in Havana Harbor. As the commander of the South Atlantic Fleet, Sampson had been pursuing Cervera to no avail, but finally he received word that his prey was taking refuge in Santiago Harbor. He left Havana immediately and deployed his ships to blockade the Santiago entrance.[20] At first he considered sailing into the harbor and destroying Cervera's fleet, as Dewey had done in Manila Bay, but the strong Spanish coastal defenses ruled that out. Sampson therefore contented himself with blockading the entrance to Santiago Harbor. As a sideshow, he sent an expedition to seize Guantánamo Bay, forty miles to the east, to establish a base. He then sent to Washington a strong recommendation that an army be sent to Santiago to reduce the Spanish coastal defenses.

In Washington President McKinley decided to comply with Sampson's recommendation. He overrode the objections of Miles, who thought the objective to be unimportant, and directed Shafter to take his Fifth Corps to Santiago.

On June 1, Sampson received word that an Army force of twenty–five thousand men was on its way.

19. Trask, *War with Spain in 1898,* 116.
20. The distance from Havana to San Juan is 1,130 miles. Ibid., 118.

6

Las Guasimas

General William Shafter's Fifth Corps was small by usual military standards; it consisted of only about sixteen thousand officers and men, twenty–three hundred horses and mules, two hundred wagons, sixteen light guns, a dozen heavier guns, and other weapons.[1] It was, however, the largest force that could be carried on the thirty–two transports available. Shafter's biggest problem was not the size of his force, but uncertainty as to his destination. Lacking specific orders, he took matters into his own hands. Presuming that he would eventually be sent to the vicinity of Santiago Bay, he followed a course around the eastern tip of Cuba and thence westward along the south coast.

Fortunately for his men, the seas were calm, somewhat alleviating the misery they were undergoing in the holds of the ships. The greatest source of distress was the heat. Many of the men, those coming from the sands of Texas, Arizona, and New Mexico, were somewhat inured to hot weather, but those from the Ivy League schools fared worse. Nevertheless, they made the best of the situation and spent their time as soldiers always do on transports: some gambled, some just gazed at the sea, and others passed the time writing letters.

Wood and Roosevelt were of course responsible for seeing to the welfare of the troops, but their actual duties did not take up much of their time. Both occupied themselves writing letters, of which Roosevelt's were the more remarkable because they hardly read like those normally expected from a lieutenant colonel far down the chain of command. On June 12, even before the *Yucatan* left Tampa, Roosevelt wrote to Senator Lodge, in which letter the lieutenant colonel gave the senator his instructions:

1. Frank Freidel, *The Splendid Little War,* 68–69, 72.

> I wonder if it would be possible for you to tell the Administration, that is, the President, and if necessary the Secretary of War, just what is going on here and the damage that is being done. Of course, I cannot speak publicly in any way; I should be court–martialed if I did, but this letter I shall show to Wood, my Colonel, and it is written after consultation with Gen. Young,[2] my brigade commander. I shall not show this first to Wood or to Young, for I want to say that it would be impossible to get a better man than Wood has shown himself to be, and so far as I am concerned I am entirely content with Young as Brigade General but otherwise the mismanagement here is frightful.[3]

He then continued on for several pages, not bothering with such conventions as paragraphs, outlining his observations of everything wrong described above and then some.

Wood's letters, on the other hand, were written almost exclusively to his wife and were more conventional. Sometimes he showed a touch of the poet, and sometimes he lapsed into gloomy reality. On June 15, the day of departure from Tampa, he wrote describing the experience of being on the ocean: "Painted ships on a painted ocean. Imagine three great lines of transports with a warship at the head of each line, steaming in long lines, 800 yards from each other over a sea of indigo blue, real deep blue, such as I have never seen before. Air warm and balmy, with a gentle breeze stirring up the water. No swell or disturbance. Simply a great peaceful marine picture." But then, on June 20: "No one seems to know exactly what we are to do or where we are to land. You can hardly imagine the awful confusion and lack of system which meets one on every hand in this business. . . . Somehow everything seems to go on in a happy–go–lucky way. . . . If the Europeans want to intervene, nothing could give them more encouragement. . . . [We are lucky] having struck a broken–down power, for we would surely have had a deuced hard time with any other."[4]

General Shafter and his staff made the trip on the *Seguranca,* along with a group of war correspondents, men who took themselves far more seriously than did the Army. Foremost among them was Richard Harding Davis, still reporting for Hearst's *New York Journal.* But there were other men of note

2. Brigadier General Samuel B. M. Young.

3. Roosevelt to Lodge, June 12, 1898, quoted in Brands, *Selected Letters of Roosevelt,* 187–88.

4. Hagedorn, *Leonard Wood, a Biography,* 1:160.

such as Stephen Crane, famed as the author of *The Red Badge of Courage.* And another, Ed Marshall, also of the *New York Journal,* was a man with an ego to compare to that of Davis. These men would play a significant role in the way the public would later perceive the war.

On June 20, the day that Wood was writing his last letter from the ship, Shafter's flotilla arrived off the mouth of Santiago Bay, in view of the great arc of American naval vessels bottling up Cervera's fleet. There he was joined aboard the *Yucatan* by Admiral Sampson, who was waiting for him. As they conferred, they realized how little they really knew of the situation ashore at Santiago. To secure solid information, they decided that they needed to confer with Calixto Garcia, the leader of the Cuban rebels in the region. So the *Yucatan* continued eighteen miles farther west, past Santiago Harbor, and landed on the beach where Garcia kept his headquarters. After the ragtag but inevitable honor guard, the three men began conferring seriously.

Garcia was an impressive–looking man, overweight but with a flowing white mustache and full goatee. Anyone meeting him for the first time was startled by the sight of a pronounced vertical crease running up his forehead, caused by a failed suicide attempt when he was being tortured by the Spanish authorities years earlier. He bore the scar proudly, to advertise his ordeal to the world. Long an effective guerrilla commander, his forces currently controlled the countryside in the center and eastern end of the island, thus cutting Spanish forces in Santiago off from those in Havana. His main mission in the forthcoming campaign, as he saw it, would be to prevent reinforcement of the Spanish garrison by troops from the western end of the island.

The meeting was conducted under pleasant circumstances under palm trees on a sandy beach, but the matters discussed were critical, for up to that time there had been no joint planning between the Army and the Navy as to how to employ Shafter's forces. From Garcia the Americans learned the dispositions of the eighty thousand or so Spanish soldiers occupying Cuba, of which only about twelve thousand were located in the vicinity of Santiago. He also had accurate information on the possible beaches where Shafter's troops might come ashore. Garcia was all cooperation; he even agreed to provide troops to help in the capture of the ground overlooking Santiago.

Fortunately, the three men agreed on their basic purpose, which was to destroy Cervera's fleet. They also recognized that Sampson could not enter Santiago Harbor under the Spanish guns overlooking the entrance. The question, then, lay in the employment of Shafter's troops. Sampson proposed that Shafter simply attack the Spanish gun positions straight on. Shafter, however, demurred. He had been doing some reading while aboard ship and had found an account of a siege of Santiago by British admiral Edward Vernon in 1741, as part of the War of Jenkins's Ear. The city had held out, principally because the attackers had been unable to scale the 230–foot cliffs. Since that episode, Shafter had learned, the Spanish had made the position even stronger by building the Morro Castle on one side and the batteries of Socapa on the other. A direct assault would be difficult, if not impossible.

As an alternative, Garcia recommended that Shafter establish a base at a town named Siboney, about six miles east of the bay, from which to follow a trail grandly called the King's Highway to San Juan Hill, a terrain feature overlooking Santiago and the bay. Possession of that hill would make the Spanish position untenable. But Siboney itself was unsatisfactory as a landing site.[5] So to reach it, Shafter was forced to land his troops at a beach, Daiquiri, that was located an additional nine miles to the east of Siboney. The march overland from Daiquiri to Siboney would be arduous, and even Daiquiri was a dangerous landing spot, but no other option existed. So Daiquiri it was.

On June 22, 1898, the landing party of Fifth Corps unloaded from their troopships at Daiquiri, expecting to be raked by Spanish fire at any moment. Considering the uncertainty of the situation and the possibility of being forced to withdraw, Shafter placed the two divisions ashore under the operational control of Major General Joseph Wheeler, commanding the Cavalry Division, as the senior officer.[6] The infantry division commander was William Lawton, Leonard Wood's friend and onetime commander. Shafter, in no physical condition to command in person, remained afloat on the *Yucatan* for the time being.

At this point, Shafter made an error that would later do much to damage his reputation with the public: he alienated the correspondents, especially Richard Harding Davis. When informed that he would not be allowed to accompany the first wave of landing troops, Davis confronted Shafter with a demand that the order be rescinded. Shafter refused. Then, when Davis claimed that he was no ordinary reporter but a "descriptive writer," Shafter did not merely stand his ground—he lost his temper.[7] Davis was one who never forgot a slight.

---

5. Guantánamo Bay, though already secured by Sampson's naval forces, was 40 miles away.

6. President McKinley had decided that one of the division commanders had to be an ex–Confederate.

7. Jack Cameron Dierks, *A Leap to Arms: The Cuban Campaign of 1898,* 84–85.

Shafter was probably unaware of just how dangerous a landing he was executing. The number of Spanish troops that he had gotten from Garcia, twelve thousand, was not too daunting, but Shafter may have underestimated how battle hardened those Spaniards were as a result of fighting the Cuban insurrections for many years. He also may or may not have realized that the enemy soldiers were better armed than the Americans; their rifles were the German Mauser, which used smokeless powder and was far superior to the American Krag–Jørgensen.[8] And finally, the landing area at Daiquiri was extremely difficult. Heights rose right behind the beach, and the waters were extremely shallow for many hundreds of yards out. The troops would be forced to leave their vessels a long ways out, and as they waded through the surf they would be highly vulnerable to fire from the shore.

But Shafter was lucky. The Cuban rebels who had joined him brought the happy news that the Spanish commander, Lieutenant General Arsenio Linares y Pombo, had timidly withdrawn from the beach, leaving only a handful of defenders. So in the morning, Shafter began his landing.[9] Miraculously, his men suffered few losses.

"Fighting Joe" Wheeler, whom Shafter had placed in tactical command of troops ashore, was the kind of man of whom legends are made. Though sometimes accused of forgetting that he was fighting Spaniards rather than Yankees, he had long since made total peace with his former foes. At the end of the Civil War, he had spent some time as a prisoner of war at Fort Monroe, Virginia (along with Jefferson Davis), in the custody of his present comrade Nelson Miles. He had soon been released, however, and had served in the US Congress for twenty years. When asked at Tampa how it felt to be wearing the blue uniform of the Union army, he had answered, "I feel as though I had been away on a three–week's furlough and had just come back to my own colors."[10]

Wheeler's Division consisted of two dismounted cavalry brigades. The 1st Brigade, under Brigadier General Samuel S. Sumner, consisted of three regu-

8. Apparently, there was no shortage of ammunition, and Mauser ammunition came to be used as legal tender in the streets of Santiago. Americans were told that prostitutes in Santiago charged for their services according to a soldier's rank: one hundred Mauser cartridges for a private, two hundred for a noncom, and a full thousand rounds from an officer. The Americans were hopeful that Krag ammunition could be used likewise. Ibid., 88.

9. Freidel, *The Splendid Little War,* 81–82.

10. Ibid., 100.

lar regiments. The 2d Brigade, under Brigadier General S. B. M. Young, also consisted of three regiments, but these were two regular and one volunteer, the Rough Riders. Roosevelt, normally a severe critic of his superiors, was delighted that the 1st Volunteer Cavalry would be assigned to Young's brigade.

Roosevelt and the general were old friends, stemming from the days when the two had been members of a hunting club at Yellowstone National Park. Young had recently visited Roosevelt at the Metropolitan Club in Washington and at that time, anticipating the coming war with Spain, had urged Wood and Roosevelt to exert every effort to join his brigade. In that case, he would "guarantee to show us fighting."[11] Now, almost miraculously, that arrangement had come to pass. Although Young had promised his friends "plenty of fighting," Wood and Roosevelt realized that the general also had two regiments of regulars under his command. Wood knew that he would have to make strong efforts to keep the Rough Riders at the front of the action.

On landing at Daiquiri Beach, the 1st Volunteer Cavalry marched about a quarter of a mile inland in order to make room for the following units. They camped in a flat area surrounded by palm trees and replete with land crabs, harmless novelties. Nearby was a pool, the odor of which ensured that it could never be used for drinking water. The men had landed with their gear, but Young, Wood, and Roosevelt, rather quixotically setting an example, carried only mackintoshes on their backs and toothbrushes in their pockets. It was well that the three had brought their mackintoshes, for they were soon drenched by a heavy tropical storm. Nevertheless, with undampened spirits, they awaited orders to move toward Siboney in the morning. With the irrational eagerness for battle shared only by new soldiers, they awaited action eagerly.

On the morning of June 23, after a miserable night at Daiquiri, Wheeler's men set out along the narrow and rocky trail to Siboney. On arrival late in the day, they met up with a detachment of Garcia's men and began setting up a base to receive supplies. By nightfall Wheeler's men had secured Siboney, and the supply ships began unloading, naked men pulling and toting, glad to be there, and cheering as they toiled. Reporter Richard Harding Davis, on viewing the men at work, thought it probably one of the strangest scenes of an unloading in history.

There was every reason for speed, because the yellow–fever season was approaching. But not everything could be done instantaneously. Even though

11. Roosevelt, *The Rough Riders,* 73–74.

Shafter was aware of the need, he still planned at least to consolidate his beachhead before moving inland. Wheeler, however, acted on his own. Without consulting Shafter, he departed Siboney the morning after arriving. His order of march, contrary to Shafter's orders, placed his own Cavalry Division in the lead. His route ran along the "King's Highway," which was not much more than a rough trail leading to the San Juan Heights, nine miles away. Cuban scouts had advised that General Linares was planning to defend a strong position a few miles inland at a place called Las Guasimas. At the moment, the Spanish line was weak, but if Linares should reinforce it with a portion of his reserves, the position would be nearly impregnable. At 5:45 on the morning of June 24, Young's brigade set out. Young, despite his promises to Wood and Roosevelt to show them battle, still preferred to send his two regular regiments, the 1st and 10th, in the lead along the main road, intending to hold the Rough Riders in reserve.

Wood and Roosevelt, however, were not to be denied. They found a secondary trail that led off to the west and then ran parallel to the main road, converging with it at Las Guasimas. Admittedly, the trail was steep and narrow, requiring the men to march single file, but it put the Rough Riders in the battle.

The first shots were fired at 8:15 a.m.—Colonel William Beach, Wheeler's chief engineer, made a special note of the time. Resistance from the Spanish was far heavier than Wheeler had expected, and their line held. So firm was their line that even the aggressive Wheeler swallowed his pride and sent a request back to Henry Lawton for infantry reinforcements.

On the trail to the west, the Rough Riders were also meeting a hail of fire from an entrenched enemy. Exhibiting contempt for the enemy bullets whizzing around him, Wood joked but managed to remain in control. At one point, he noticed a shiny piece of metal lying at his feet. On picking it up, he found that an enemy bullet had grazed his left wrist, passing through his sleeve and shattering his cuff link. Roosevelt fared worse; a shell hit the palm tree above his head, sending splinters that penetrated his ears and superficially his eye, though his vision was unimpaired.

Wood was handling things masterfully. He had hit the enemy line with five of his eight troops abreast with three held in reserve. On discovery that the Spanish position was slightly wider than his attacking front, however, he employed two of his reserve troops, one on each flank, and put Roosevelt in control of the right of his line.

The Rough Riders' action was well reported, because the newspaper reporters had decided to accompany them. The most influential was Richard

Harding Davis, who had already reported on enough of the Latin American revolutions from Spain that he was the most battlewise man on the spot. He set aside his notepad long enough to point out enemy positions to Wood. At one point, he even picked up a Krag and fired a few shots. Wood later mentioned Davis lavishly in his reports, and Davis reciprocated, thus much affecting the public's perception of what had happened in the Santiago campaign.

Finally, Wood committed his last remaining troop on his left, in what has since come to be called "Wood's Bluff." The psychological effect of this attack emanated not from its strength but from its weakness; the Spanish commander could not believe that Wood's attack was being made by the last of the troops. The Spaniard saw it as the vanguard of another regiment.

Everything came together at once. The Rough Riders converged with the regulars at Las Guasimas at about the same time as an infantry battalion from the 6th Infantry, sent by Lawton. The Spanish line retreated, slowly at first, then faster, finally degenerating into flight. Las Guasimas, the strongest defensive position available to Linares, was in American hands. Wheeler, who was at the front, stood up and yelled, "We've got the Yankees on the run!" Colonel Beach checked his watch; the battle had lasted only a little over an hour.

It had been only a skirmish, but it had been costly. The Americans lost fifteen men killed and fifty–two wounded. The Spanish losses were somewhat less: ten killed and twenty–five wounded.[12] Although all the losses were mourned, Roosevelt was particularly aggrieved by the deaths of both Sergeant Hamilton Fish and Captain Allyn Capron Jr. In writing his account of the Rough Riders, Roosevelt had these laudatory remarks to say:

> Hamilton Fish had already shown himself to be one of the best non–commissioned officers we had. A huge fellow, of enormous strength and endurance and dauntless courage, he took naturally to the soldier's life. He never complained and never shirked any duty of any kind, while his power over his men was great. As we stood around the flickering fire that night [of July 23], I caught myself admiring the splendid bodily vigor of Capron and Fish—the captain and the sergeant. Capron was going over his plans for the fight when we should meet the Spaniards on the morrow, Fish occasionally asking a question. They were both filled with eager longing to show their mettle. Within twelve hours they both were dead.[13]

12. Freidel, *The Splendid Little War,* 115.
13. Roosevelt, *The Rough Riders,* 79–80.

Once dislodged from their position along the Las Guasimas Ridge, the Spaniards offered no more resistance. They fled back into their main defenses on San Juan Hill, leaving the Americans free to move around the area. Shafter came ashore and set up camp at the town of Sevilla, a spot that provided relatively flat ground, adequate water supply, and natural defenses. Here the Americans would have time to rest. The men and horses were exhausted and disorganized. Shafter set out to make preparations for the next move on the San Juan Heights.

Las Guasimas can arguably be considered as Leonard Wood's finest performance on the battlefield. Once he discovered that Linares intended to fight on that ridgeline, he quickly adjusted his dispositions and exercised remarkable personal leadership. Though aware of the danger from enemy Mausers, he exposed himself to enemy fire, not as an act of showmanship, but to keep an eye on the way the battle was developing. Occasionally, when the fighting was thickest, he would make a small joke to whoever happened to be near. He noted both bravery and cowardice. He forbade swearing among his troops even under the most trying conditions.

Wood's sole concern was the good of his regiment, and at one point that concern caused him to show a surprising tolerance for an act of cowardice. In one instance, an officer—all accounts spare us his name—disgraced himself. He had always been unnecessarily strict and therefore highly unpopular among the Rough Riders, even as far back as the days at San Antonio. His was the type of personality that sagacious men would predict cowardice. When the battle was at its peak, a trooper named McIlhenny, just out of a sickbed, was struggling up the hill to rejoin his unit when he heard the sound of hooves heading for the rear. On turning he soon realized that the fleeing figure riding was none other than the martinet himself. McIlhenny yelled out, asking where the officer was going.

The story the officer told McIlhenny was convincing and alarming. The regiment had been "cut to pieces," he claimed. Wood had been killed and Roosevelt wounded. He himself, he insisted, was heading for Siboney to bring up reinforcements. McIlhenny had no excuse to delay him, and he continued on.

None of the officer's reports, of course, turned out to be true, but they could have been. This was the moment when Wheeler himself had sent back to Lawton for help. And it was then that Wood made his critical last attack, his "bluff," that won the day.

The deserter, however, had not gotten away with his conduct. Word got around, and soon every man was in on the facts. The Rough Riders had among them a tough gang of men, and for a while it appeared that the onetime martinet had a justifiable cause to fear for his life. But Wood took no action against him. Sensing the resentment of all the troopers, Captain William Llewellyn, the senior troop commander, confronted Wood, announcing that he intended to submit an official complaint of cowardice.

Wood knew that Llewellyn was absolutely correct in his judgment and his legal prerogative. He frankly admitted to the captain that he and his associates could take that action. But then he gave his own viewpoint: that he hoped the captain would not take action. He pointed out that the eyes of the country were on the Rough Riders, and if a court–martial for cowardice were to be held, it would reflect on the entire regiment. The result would be that the heroism exhibited by so many would be forgotten. Llewellyn gave in with an ominous warning that this officer would run away in every fight in the future.

Wood may have been amused by Llewellyn's anger, but he took no action. He was already becoming sophisticated in the ways of the American press.[14]

The most immediate problem now facing Shafter was supply, especially of food. The rations, which at best were not very appetizing, were made less so by the poor quality of the beef, which was inedible. Hungry though the men were, most of them threw their meat ration away. Next priority was the evacuation of the wounded; fortunately, the same mules could be used for both evacuation and resupply in their round–trips from Siboney.

Other items of supply were also urgent. It was necessary, of course, to give top priority to ammunition and guns. The task was slow; the small port of Siboney was totally inadequate, and the supplies as loaded on the ships were disorganized. Each crate had to be opened before its contents could be identified. Add to that the deplorable condition of the King's Highway, and it is understandable why it took time for Shafter to build up a level of supply to sustain an all–out attack on Santiago.

In the meantime, important changes were occurring in the command structure of Fifth Corps. General Wheeler came down with a fever and was replaced by General Sumner as commander of the Cavalry Division. That development improved the team. Wheeler was a colorful man, but his judgment was sometimes a cause for doubt. Even his admirers admit that his aggressiveness brought on the unnecessary Battle of Las Guasimas. Had he been less impetuous in attacking Las Gausimas, Linares would probably have retired from the position anyway. But Wheeler's rash action had one good result. The

14. Hagedorn, *Leonard Wood, a Biography,* 1:168–71.

experience the Americans had gained in that one–hour battle at Las Guasimas was invaluable when it came to sterner fights ahead.

Another change in the Cavalry Division affected Roosevelt and Wood more directly: Wood was elevated to command Young's Brigade when the latter fell sick with a fever. Both Roosevelt and Wood were happy with their promotions. As brigade commander, Wood would receive the coveted star of a brigadier general. Perhaps just as important to him was the honor of being so selected despite the fact of his status as a volunteer. He was now assured, he wrote his wife, that his promotion would not be a matter of being "kicked upstairs" under pressure from politicians in Washington. His elevation had been based on his stellar performance at Las Guasimas.

Roosevelt was even more delighted. Without expressing an ounce of regret at the departure of Wood from the regiment, he later wrote,

> General Young was struck down with the fever, and Wood took charge of the brigade. This left me in command of the regiment, of which I was very glad, for such experience as we had had is a quick teacher. By this time the men and I knew one another, and I felt able to make them do themselves justice in march or battle. They understood that I paid no heed to where they came from; no heed to their creed, politics, or social standing; that I care for them to the utmost of my power, but that I demanded the highest performance of duty; while in return I had seen them tested, and I knew I could depend absolutely on their courage, hardihood, obedience, and individual initiative.[15]

Roosevelt's self–congratulation aside, the change made little difference in the relationship between Roosevelt and Wood. Wood remained Roosevelt's immediate superior, only at a higher level. The two men continued to bunk together in bivouac. There was plenty of glory to go around.

15. Roosevelt, *The Rough Riders,* 108.

7

San Juan Hill

The charge up San Juan Hill and its flanking outpost, Kettle Hill, seemed in 1898 to be one of the most heroic deeds in American military history. It crowned with luster the military reputation of one of its chief participants, Theodore Roosevelt, who in little more than three years became president of the United States. As years went by, the blundering inefficiency of the high command overshadowed the courageous hardihood of the troops; the energetic resistance of the Spaniards was forgotten. In the retelling, the battle seemed something of a skylark, almost comic in nature, obscuring the grim and desperate struggle that bloody day.[1]

Once General William Shafter had debarked from the *Seguranca* and assumed direct command of his corps, he lost no time in looking over the terrain between his headquarters and San Juan Hill. In so doing, he established an observation post on a key hillock named El Pozo, on the main road to Santiago.

While he was visiting El Pozo, Shafter ran into an odd figure, very much out of place. Riding a large white horse and wearing a broad straw hat and crumpled white suit, the figure turned out to be William Randolph Hearst himself, a man who had done so much to bring this war about. Hearst had sailed to Cuba aboard his luxurious private yacht, accompanied by a horde of reporters in a follow–up boat. Getting a firsthand view of the prospective battlefield was his professed purpose, but the reporters would provide publicity. Hearst also much desired to interview Shafter, and it was probably no accident that he appeared at El Pozo at the same time as the general.

1. Freidel, *The Splendid Little War,* 143.

Shafter welcomed his visitor. Putting aside the animosity he usually bore toward reporters, he treated the press magnate with a courtesy he had not shown Davis at Daiquiri. Hearst reciprocated by painting Shafter in the most favorable light possible, describing the obese old general as "a bold, lion–headed hero, massive as to body—a sort of human fortress in blue coat and flannel shirt."[2]

Shafter knew that time was not on his side. On June 28, Cuban irregulars had brought word that about eight thousand Spanish troops were on the way to Santiago and had reached a point about forty–five miles off to the west. There were other reasons to act soon. Resupply had been accomplished, and the troops were becoming restless. Regardless of the dangers that lay ahead, everyone wanted to get on with it. Shafter therefore gave the order that he planned to break camp on July 30 and attack the approaches to Santiago on July 1.

El Pozo was more than an observation post; it was also a key road junction between two main roads. One was the Santiago Road that led to the base of the San Juan Heights about two miles away, about a mile of which was concealed by a dense jungle. Another road ran northward to a small town named El Caney, about four miles away. It was potentially a strong position; even at that distance, Shafter could make out a couple of blockhouses and a fort south of it. But Shafter was optimistic; Garcia's men had advised him that El Caney was probably being occupied by only a few Spanish troops. Garcia thought it to be merely outposted.

Shafter's contempt for his enemy caused him to split his forces. Because the road that ran westward to the San Juan River was so difficult, he would try to envelop Santiago by way of El Caney. Lawton's 2d Division would move northward and seize the town and then turn south to hit the Spanish position on San Juan Heights. The rest of the corps, General Samuel S. Sumner's (Wheeler's) Cavalry Division leading, would start out westward from El Pozo only after receiving word that El Caney had fallen to Lawton. Sumner, with Kent following, would then take the road westward through the jungle to the San Juan River.[3] Across the San Juan River, where the approaches to the San Juan Heights covered open country, the two divisions would take separate routes.

2. Walker, *Boys of '98,* 199–200.

3. Major General Jacob L. Kent's First Division made a forced march from Siboney by June 30. Eventually, it was visualized that the two divisions would both be on the main road, each division on a side of the road.

The plan has since been criticized by military analysts, who possess information not available to Shafter, for depending so heavily on the El Caney attack. However, Shafter justified it, with some reason, because the alternative, the direct route, would be miserable. There was no reason not to believe Garcia, who had advised that El Caney was merely outposted. Lawton's 2d Division, reinforced to reach a total of about 6,550 men, should take El Caney in a couple of hours at the most.

Shafter issued orders to his subordinates at his headquarters during the early afternoon of June 30. A couple of hours later, Lawton had his men on the road toward El Caney. So confident of success was Shafter that he assigned Lawton only two light artillery batteries, one of them commanded by Captain Allyn Capron Sr., who had lost his son at Las Guasimas but was determined to play his role despite the shock of the young officer's death.

That afternoon of June 30, shortly after his final meeting, Shafter came down sick, overcome by the heat, his corpulence, and the strenuous activities of the past few days. He retired to his tent at Los Mangos and directed the battle—to the extent it was directed—by sending orders through his aide. He was lucid, and his judgment was unimpaired. But personal supervision was lacking.

According to plan, Lawton bivouacked near El Caney on the evening of June 30 and by 9:00 the next morning began his attack on the town. As soon as the first shots were fired, Lawton realized that the enemy position, instead of being merely outposted, was fortified. Infantry foxholes blocked the approaches, along with barbed-wire entanglements. A stone fort, five hundred yards southeast of town, with a supporting blockhouse, was a strong position.[4] To make matters more serious, coordination among Lawton's units was poor. At one point, Capron's artillery battery fired on a column of friendly Cuban *insurrectos.* It also proved that the four light artillery pieces were totally incapable of penetrating either the stone fort or the blockhouse. The Americans had also failed to take into account the quality of the Spanish commander, General Joaquin Vara del Rey, who had every intention of defending El Caney to the death.

Because neither side possessed anything like adequate artillery support, the battle degenerated into one almost entirely between infantrymen. In this the German Mauser in the hands of the Spaniards took a fearsome toll. At 10:00 a.m., Lawton called a halt to the attack to allow his exhausted men a chance to rest.

4. Freidel, *The Splendid Little War,* 126.

Three hours later, at 1:00 p.m., Lawton ordered the action resumed. By now his ten–to–one advantage in troop strength told, and by 2:30 p.m. the Americans were at the edge of the town. At this point, an impatient General Shafter sent Lawton an order to move on the town, ignoring the blockhouses. Too late; Lawton was already assaulting them at great cost. But the time had come. General Vara del Rey was finally shot down, and without his leadership the defenders quickly surrendered. But it was 4:00 p.m., late in the day.

Despite the intensity of the fighting—or perhaps because of it—both sides admired the courage of their adversaries. While the Americans were burying General Vara del Rey with full military honors, one Spanish officer expressed his feelings succinctly: "I have never seen anything to equal the courage of those Americans, who, stripped to the waist, offering their breasts to our murderous fire, literally threw themselves on our trenches—on the muzzles of their guns. We had the advantage of position, and mowed them down by the hundreds; but they never retreated or fell back an inch. As one man fell, shot through the heart, another would take his place, with grim determination and unflinching devotion to duty in every line of his face. Their gallantry was heroic."[5]

The cost had been heavy. The Americans had suffered 441 total casualties, of which 81 were deaths. The losses of the Spaniards came to only 235 killed and wounded, with the loss of 120 men as prisoners. But that was more than half their strength.

The most important aspect of the attack on El Caney was the unexpected delay it had caused to Shafter's plans for the move on Santiago. He was forced to launch his main attack with only part of his force, and through the jungle.

In the absence of the personal direction that only Shafter himself could have provided,[6] Sumner and Kent were left to decide the plan of attack themselves. At 11:00 a.m., with no word from Lawton, the two conferred, and as a

5. Ibid., 138–39.

6. Roosevelt's account: "Immediately our guns opened, and at the report great clouds of white smoke hung on the [Pozo] ridge crest. Wood and I were sitting together, and Wood remarked to me that he wished our brigade could be moved somewhere else, for we were directly in line of any return fire by the Spaniards at the battery. Hardly had he spoken when there was a peculiar whistling, singing sound in the air, and immediately afterward the noise of something exploding above our heads. It was shrapnel from the Spanish batteries. We sprung to our feet and leaped on our horses. Immediately afterward a second shot came which burst over us; and then a third. . . . I at once hustled my regiment over the crest of the hill into the thick underbrush, where I had no little difficulty in getting them together again into column." Roosevelt, *The Rough Riders*, 116.

result they set out on the jungle trail that led directly to the San Juan River and the heights beyond. Although the distance was only a bit more than a mile, the troops were confined to a narrow trail. On arrival at the river, the Americans faced the San Juan Heights, with San Juan Hill to the left (south) and Kettle Hill on the right (north). By prior plan, Sumner's Cavalry Division was to turn right, deploying at the base of Kettle Hill. Kent's 1st Infantry Division would turn left and deploy at the base of San Juan Hill.

The plan sounded simple, but its execution was extremely difficult. The trail was narrow, and the heat was in the nineties. The regular troops were wearing the stifling woolen uniforms that Roosevelt described as "exactly what I would have worn in Montana in the fall."[7] Further, with two divisions, totaling eight regiments, along a single trail, movement was slow. It was, in the words of Richard Harding Davis, like "fifteen regiments encamped along the sidewalks of Fifth Avenue and were all ordered at the same moment to move into it and march downtown."[8] The density of the jungle made it impossible to see where they were going. Fortunately, an observer in a barrage balloon raised near the ford over the San Juan River discovered a small trail that ran parallel to the main road. Kent made use of it and was able to move up abreast with Sumner.

Finally, Sumner's men reached the ford and made the planned right turn, along the bank of the San Juan River. The fire was heavy. At that point, a horrified Roosevelt saw Bucky O'Neill fall dead, shot through the heart. Moments before, O'Neill had boasted that the Spanish bullet that would kill him had not been cast. Many others met the same fate, partly because the observation balloon that had spotted Kent's trail now showed the Spanish the position of American troops.

Kent's division, on the left, also came under intense fire. Particularly hard hit was the 71st New York Volunteer Infantry, totally inexperienced and equipped with antiquated Springfield rifles, the smoke of which was worse than that of the Krag. The men of the 71st refused to move forward when ordered and finally pulled back, thus placing volunteer troops higher in the contempt of the regulars.

For some reason, Wood, as brigade commander, did not place the Rough Riders in the vanguard of his formation. Instead, he placed Roosevelt and his men behind the two regular cavalry regiments, the 1st and the 10th. Neverthe-

7. Dierks, *Leap to Arms*, 97.

8. Ibid., 97. He adds that Davis neglected to mention that the Fifth Avenue in question was only fifteen feet wide.

less, with the other regiments moving so slowly, the Rough Riders were soon in the worst of it. Once across the San Juan River, Roosevelt's men deployed at the foot of Kettle Hill, he found his situation untenable. There was no cover or concealment, and the fire from the Spanish Mausers was heavy. Still mounted on his horse "Texas," Roosevelt rode up and down the line shouting encouragement and putting his men in place. He did not, however, possess authority to order an attack up the hill. To obtain authority from Wood, he sent four messengers, at different times, to obtain that permission. In the meantime, he lost men.

Finally, orders came to attack. Roosevelt's troopers moved forward, scrambling up the rough terrain and cheering. Roosevelt, still on horseback, urged his men on, and once they were all in motion he rode forward. By this time, the two regular cavalry regiments and the Rough Riders had become hopelessly intermingled. A few yards from the crest of Kettle Hill, Roosevelt encountered a barbed–wire fence. He released his mount and proceeded on foot.

Once on the move, the intermingled group of regular cavalry and Rough Riders quickly reached the Spanish trenches, and the Spanish, seeing that they were outnumbered about ten to one, gave way. Nobody knows exactly which unit or individual reached the crest of Kettle Hill first—nor does it matter. The Americans, through bravery, and assisted by incredible mismanagement on the part of Spain's General Linares, had carried the day. Roosevelt had led his men with gallantry, if not recklessness, and his admiring reporter, Davis, further embellished his exploits. But other units had suffered even heavier losses than had Roosevelt's. The 10th Cavalry, for example, had lost ten of its officers killed, out of a total of twenty.

Yet the battle was not quite over. From the crest of Kettle Hill, Roosevelt looked southward and discovered that Kent's infantrymen had not yet quite cleared the Spanish position atop the nearby San Juan Hill. Shouting orders to follow him, Roosevelt took off. After he had gone only about a hundred yards, however, he realized that only five men had followed him. Infuriated, he returned. As he described the episode, "After running about a hundred yards I found I had only five men with me. There was no use going on, and I ran back, jumped over the wire fence, and went over the crest of the hill, filled with anger. [W]hile I taunted them bitterly for not having followed me, it was all I could do not to smile at the look of injury and surprise that came over their faces, while they cried out, 'We didn't hear you, we didn't see you go, Colonel, lead on now, we'll surely follow you.'"[9]

9. Roosevelt, *The Rough Riders,* 134.

Roosevelt, by his own account, then consulted quickly with General Sumner, who placed all the troopers in the vicinity of Kettle Hill under Roosevelt's personal command. At about that time, however, San Juan Hill fell to Kent, very largely because of the arrival of a new weapon—or at least a new use for a weapon already in the inventory: the Gatling gun.

The Gatling gun had been very much the project of Lieutenant John H. Parker, a young West Pointer from the class of 1892, who possessed a vision lacking in the higher reaches of command. It was the forerunner of the machine gun, a cylinder of a dozen barrels that fired in sequence as a gunner turned a crank and the barrel rotated. Amazingly, a single gun could fire thirty thousand rounds a minute, making a sound that Roosevelt himself described as "chunkachunkachunka." Parker's battery consisted of four such guns, and when he finally got them to the base of San Juan Hill, after floating them on rafts and dragging them over brutal terrain, they took only a few minutes to disperse the Spanish troops atop San Juan Hill. By the time Roosevelt and his men arrived on the scene, the enemy had gone.

All this had transpired under Leonard Wood, who was in command of the brigade. At the time that Parker's Gatlings opened fire at the juncture of the Santiago Road and the San Juan River, Wood was with him, coordinating the actions of his brigade with that of Sumner's other brigade on his left. That accomplished, Wood started out accompanying Parker as he moved up San Juan Hill. A second thought hit him: he should check on his right flank at Kettle Hill. On arrival at that position, he found his right flank hanging in the air. The road from El Caney, where Lawton was still fighting desperately, was open. Spanish troops could come down that road and hit him from that direction, creating a disaster.

Wood took immediate action. He sent a messenger to Sumner, urgently asking for additional guns to be sent up at once. He then went in person down the hill to find infantry reinforcements. Because the disorganized infantry could offer no help, Wood sought out the Gatlings, ordering an exhausted Parker to move to the crest of Kettle Hill. The right flank of the brigade and the corps were now protected.

It was none too soon. A mass of some five hundred Spanish soldiers had been preparing to do what Wood had feared, to hit his right flank. When they came under the fire of the Gatlings, however, they melted away. But some of Wood's men were still in some peril, having zealously pushed forward ahead of the strongest position. An infantry officer asked Wood's permission to withdraw to safer ground, but Wood refused. As Davis described the scene, "He had no uniform, no sword. He wore khaki riding breeches and a gray shirt and carried a riding crop. 'Get back [forward] Boys,' he said quietly, pointing with his crop. 'Get back. The others won't understand. Get back.' And they instantly got back and stayed there. It was one of the best examples I ever saw of the power of one man's authority upon disciplined troops without the insignia of rank to prove it."[10] Davis may have been exaggerating the effect of what a man wore on his shoulders, but there was no question of either Wood's bravery or his concern for the effects of one man's actions on the morale of the rest.

The enemy was on the run, but the exhausted Americans did not pursue; they were happy enough to stay in place. Shafter had to give up his original hope of continuing on and taking Santiago that day. Besides the prevalent exhaustion, Spanish defenses between San Juan Hill and Santiago were found to be even stronger than those already taken. So that was it for the day.

The attack on San Juan and Kettle Hills had been made by only a little more than half of Shafter's force because one of his divisions, Lawton's, was not there. When Lawton finished reducing El Caney at about 4:00 p.m., he thought it too risky to continue the attack southward through unknown territory with night coming on. He therefore marched his 2d Division all the way back to El Pozo and followed the trail previously used by the main force. The next day, he took position near the north end of Santiago Harbor on the right of Sumner.

The historic assault on San Juan Heights was complete.

10. Hagedorn, *Leonard Wood, a Biography,* 1:179.

8

The Surrender of Santiago

Though Shafter's men had seized San Juan Heights, the Spaniards were by no means finished. The men previously atop the hill had merely dropped back and entrenched themselves in a strong reverse–slope position only three hundred yards away. The exhausted Americans had suffered heavier casualties than had the defenders, and the Americans bore the burden of caring for the wounded[1] and removing them down the hill to the makeshift hospital at Siboney. The rough trail made it necessary to use several able–bodied men to carry a single casualty. So many men taken out of the front lines meant that the line of American defenders of the San Juan Heights was thin indeed.

Supply was critically short, and resupply was a slow process. Despite the needs of the men, Shafter was forced to give priority to ammunition and entrenching tools over food. Water was scarce, and signs of the tropical diseases of the season had begun to set in.

As a result of these considerations, many competent officers, who could not be called timid, believed that San Juan Hill should be abandoned and the force removed back to the Sevilla plateau. Wheeler, who had returned to command the Cavalry Division, was not one of them. Nor was Wood. Nor was Roosevelt. Nor was First Lieutenant John J. Pershing of the 10th Cavalry, who declared, "We can hold this line against the whole Spanish Army." Shafter himself was torn, but for the moment, at least, he decided to hold his present position. "Hold the ground where you are until night," he ordered Wheeler.[2]

1. In civilized warfare, it is more desirable to wound an enemy soldier than to kill him.
2. Freidel, *The Splendid Little War,* 175.

A temporary disadvantage for the Americans lay in their lack of heavy artillery. Damaging the Spaniards in Santiago was so desirable that Shafter ordered a few artillery pieces, located at El Pozo, dragged up to the front lines. The project failed. Lacking direct observation of the city, the guns were forced to fire almost without targets. The smoke they emitted revealed their positions whenever they fired. In a few moments after a piece fired, incoming fire from Spanish artillery would cause everyone to take cover. The pieces were soon returned to their former position at El Pozo.

By the morning of July 3, Shafter was desperate enough that he sent a message to Secretary of War Alger, describing the situation in detail and asking for instructions: should he continue to occupy San Juan Hill, or should he pull back? Alger wisely left the final decision in Shafter's hands, adding only that it would be advantageous to morale at home if Shafter's troops could remain in his position on San Juan Heights.

The responsibility now squarely on his own shoulders, Shafter then resorted to the time–honored practice of holding a council of war. Wood, now promoted to the grade of temporary brigadier general, listened to all the logical arguments advocating withdrawal and found them unconvincing. When it came time for him to speak, therefore, he did so bluntly. "What we need here," he declared, "is less brains and more guts."[3] Whether Wood's outburst was actually decisive, Shafter eventually decided to hold his present position. At the same time, he doubled his efforts to bring about the surrender of the city without further fighting. The eleven thousand effectives of Fifth Corps remained in place on San Juan Heights.

Meanwhile, dramatic events were also taking place in Santiago. On the night of July 2, Admiral Pascual Cervera, whose fleet had now been in the harbor since May 19, received orders from Havana that he did not like. Madrid had placed him under the overall command of Captain General Ramón Blanco in Havana, who was given the title of governor of Cuba. Cervera could see that Blanco had no understanding for the naval situation across the island at Santiago. Despite Cervera's protests, Blanco believed that American occupation of San Juan Hill now made Cervera's situation untenable. The admiral, he ordered, should break out of Santiago Harbor. Cervera also suspected that Blanco placed more weight on Spanish military "honor" than on saving

3. Apparently, Wood had come by this position after much soul–searching. Frank E. Vandiver, *Black Jack: The Life and Times of John J. Pershing,* 1:206.

the lives of Cervera's sailors. But Cervera, even though angry, felt obligated to obey. The decision as to how to accomplish the escape was his.

Cervera was certain that any sortie from the protection of Santiago Harbor would be suicidal, as his four major ships and two torpedo boats were vastly outgunned by Admiral Sampson's American force. In pondering his problem, Cervera for a while considered attempting a sortie at night. He rejected that idea, however, because he knew that the shoals in Santiago Harbor were too tricky. Even if his ships were guided by expert pilots, it would be impossible to reach open waters without running aground. In addition, the searchlights on the American ships covered the area well.

Cervera therefore decided to attempt a desperate ploy designed to minimize the loss of life. Instead of heading out into open seas, he chose to turn his fleet westward through a gap he had detected in the American line;[4] keeping his ships close to shore might help a portion of the crew of any disabled vessel to escape. Before his planned breakout, he sent ashore all his official documents, papers that could be of use to the Spanish government.

Cervera burst out of the harbor on the morning of July 3, catching the Americans by surprise. It was a routine Sunday morning, with regular church services scheduled aboard all ships. Sampson himself was absent, visiting a worried General Shafter, taking with him the armored cruiser USS *New York* and two other ships. He sent two ships[5] to Guantánamo Bay for refueling. That left only the battleships *Oregon, Iowa,* and *Texas,* along with the cruiser *Brooklyn,* guarding the harbor of Santiago. In his absence, Sampson had left Rear Admiral Winfield Scott Schley in command.

At 8:45 in the morning, Cervera's fleet came out of Santiago Bay at full speed. Cervera himself was aboard his flagship, the *Maria Teresa,* followed by the *Viszcaya,* then the *Cristobal Colon,* and the *Almirante Oquendo* and the two torpedo boats. If singularly lucky, Cervera hoped, some of the ships might be able to make it westward to the port of Cienfuegos. As the fleet debouched into the open sea, the captain of the *Maria Teresa* had sad thoughts, which he later recorded: "The sound of my bugles was the last echo of those which history tells us were sounded at the capture of Granada. . . . Spain was becoming a nation of the fourth class. 'Poor Spain,' I said to my noble and beloved admiral, and he answered by an expressive motion, as though to say that he had done everything possible to avoid it."[6]

4. It was created by the absence of the *New York,* which had taken Sampson off to confer with Shafter.

5. The battleship USS *Massachusetts* and one other.

6. Freidel, *The Splendid Little War,* 194.

Cervera had another tactic for saving some of his ships, even though it involved extraordinary risk to himself. After exiting the harbor, he turned the *Maria Teresa* eastward and headed for the nearest American ship, the *Brooklyn,* in an effort to distract the attention of Schley's fleet away from the others. It did not work. Schley's men saw the *Maria Teresa* coming and realized that Cervera was apparently attempting to ram. "Then head for them," Schley commanded.

Cervera was doomed. All of Schley's ships made short work of the *Maria Teresa,* destroying it quickly. Soon the other Spanish ships were also taken under fire, their own shells hitting beyond the Americans. The smoke became so dense that the greatest danger to the Americans became the possibility of ramming one another. As described by the captain of the *Texas,* "The smoke from our guns began to hang so heavily and densely over the ship that for a few minutes we could see nothing. Suddenly a whiff of breeze and a lull in the firing lifted the pall, and there, bearing toward us and across our bows, was the *Brooklyn.* She seemed so near that it took our breath away. . . . Had the *Brooklyn* struck us then, it would probably have been the end of the *Texas* and her half–thousand men."[7]

The battle lasted for four and a half hours, and at the end every ship of the Spanish fleet was destroyed. About 450 Spanish sailors died in the action, with the loss of only a single American. The surviving Spanish sailors were made prisoners. The Americans rescued as many of the survivors as possible. Admiral Cervera was one of the fortunate ones. Taken on the *Gloucester,* he was soon transferred to the *Iowa,* whose crew had witnessed Cervera's futile attempt to save the bulk of his ships: "When [Admiral Cervera] stepped on the main deck [of the *Iowa*] he was received with all the honors according to his rank by my whole staff. The crew of the 'Iowa' together with the ones from the 'Gloucester' broke into a 'hurrah!' when the admiral saluted the American officers." And then, carried away with emotion, Evans added, "Sir, you are a hero. You have done the most sublime feat ever recorded in the history of the Navy."

For Cervera, the episode ended happily, despite his grief at losing so many men. Though sent to the United States as a prisoner of war, he was treated with honor, being housed at the United States Naval Academy. There he became an instant celebrity, often feted, and the object of requests for autographs. Offered his freedom on the condition of promising not to fight anymore in the war, he refused; the Spanish government, he insisted, would

7. Ibid., 203.

never tolerate such an action. A few days later, he was granted his freedom unconditionally.[8]

The Americans, in destroying Cervera's fleet, had cut Cuba completely in half. General Linares, commanding in Santiago, was completely isolated. Spain's prospects in Cuba were hopeless.

It was then that General Shafter demonstrated a talent for negotiation that did much to compensate for his lack of personal battlefield direction. At 10:00 on the morning of July 3, even before learning that Cervera's fleet had been destroyed, he sent a message under a flag of truce to General José Toral, who had temporarily replaced the wounded General Linares as the Spanish commander in Santiago. In something of a bluff, Shafter threatened to destroy Santiago with artillery fire from the San Juan Heights. At the same time, however, he declared a cease–fire, to remain in effect until noon the next day. During that time, foreigners, women, and children could leave the city. Those noncombatants were to leave by way of the road to El Caney, where they would be cared for pending the outcome of the siege.

Toral, in the Spanish tradition that placed honor on a pedestal above military skill, could never be expected to accept Shafter's ultimatum without orders from above, even if he were so inclined. His answer, therefore, was predictable: "The city will not surrender," he declared, "[but] I will inform the foreign consuls and inhabitants of your message." The exodus began immediately, but by noon of the next day it was apparent that a single day would not be enough. Shafter therefore extended the cease–fire for twenty–four hours, to noon on July 5.

The refugees made a pitiful sight. As Lieutenant Pershing, of the 10th Cavalry, described the scene:

> All day along the hot, dusty road leading from Santiago to El Caney, passed the long, white line; frail, hungry women carried a bundle of clothing, a parcel of food or an infant, while weak and helpless children trailed weakly at the skirts of their wretched mothers. An old man tottered along on his cane and behind him a puny lad helped an aged woman; old and young, women, children, and decrepit men of every class—those refined and used to luxury, together with the ragged beggar—crowded each other in the ragged column. It was a pitiful sight; from daylight until dark the miserable procession trooped past. The suffering of the innocent is not the least of the horrors of war.[9]

8. http://www.spanamwar.com/cervera.htm.
9. Freidel, *The Splendid Little War*, 237–38.

At El Caney, the refugees were assembled at the church, which had first been converted into a hospital by the Spanish and kept in service by the Americans. Fortunately, the Red Cross was able to provide an estimated fifteen thousand people with some medical care and, with the aid of Shafter's wagons, about eight tons of food.

Shafter then took his next step. In a second message to Toral, he offered to add the seriously wounded Spanish prisoners still held by the Americans. Toral accepted immediately, and soon twenty–seven ambulances carried wounded Spanish soldiers into Santiago. Besides the humanitarian aspect of the gesture, he expected the prisoners to spread the word among the Santiago garrison of the decent treatment they had received. Shafter thereby hoped to allay fears of American cruelty if Santiago were to be surrendered.

Shafter's overtures had the desired effect. Toral reciprocated by returning some high–profile American prisoners to Shafter's custody. He did not have many soldiers to return, but he did have some sailors, the survivors of a sunken American ship.[10] When the Americans on San Juan Heights saw the captured crew being returned, they rose to a man, doffed their weather–beaten hats, and bowed while the band played "The Star–Spangled Banner." These gestures showed that there was obviously no serious animosity between Spaniards and Americans, the men of both sides living under insufferable conditions.[11] In the course of these transactions, the cease–fire had been extended an additional day, to July 6.

Promising as these actions were, they did not impress Colonel Theodore Roosevelt, who on July 7 wrote to that effect to his friend Lodge. He began the letter with a suggestion that both he (Roosevelt) and Wood had earned promotions in the recent San Jan fight. Then he began a tirade:

> [It] is criminal to keep Shafter in command. He is utterly inefficient, and now he is panic struck. Wheeler is an old dear, but is little more fit than Shafter to command. Our part of the battle fought itself under the brigade and regimental commanders. Sumner deserves more credit than Wheeler for it—but as I say the regiments themselves really fought it. The mismanagement has been beyond belief. We are half starved; and our men are sickening daily. The lack of transportation, food and artillery has brought us to the very

10. It was a failed attempt by Admiral Sampson to block the Santiago Harbor by sinking an antiquated American rust bucket, the *Merrimac,* in its entrance.

11. Freidel, *The Splendid Little War,* 240–41. Word of the rescue of these men by the Spanish—including the participation of Admiral Cervera himself—had done much to bring about the royal treatment the admiral received upon his capture.

> verge of disaster; but above all the lack of any leadership, of any system or any executive capacity.[12]

Roosevelt had obviously not forgotten his own ambitions in fighting for the cause and the suffering of the men in the trenches. Nor was he inhibited by the strictures against jumping channels to criticize his superior. Such inhibitions were all right for regulars, but had no application to him.

Aside from the impropriety of Roosevelt's so bypassing his superiors, he was also misinformed. Shafter may not have been a battlefield leader, but neither was he stupid. Nor was he in any panic. He was simply playing his cards shrewdly to secure a surrender of Santiago without further bloodshed.

On July 8, Shafter's efforts showed signs of being rewarded: Toral informed him that Madrid had granted him permission to evacuate Santiago, provided he was allowed to do so without being attacked. A happy Shafter asked permission of Washington to accept. To his disappointment, Alger turned him down: "Your message that Spanish troops be permitted to evacuate . . . is not approved."[13] Shafter therefore passed the word to Toral that the cease–fire would end on July 10. The American troops on the hills now surrounding three sides of the city, suffering though they were, were delighted. To them, diplomacy and negotiations were tantamount to inaction.

In the meantime, however, the American situation improved. Reinforcements arrived, accompanied by General Miles, who had come in person to replace Shafter. After conferring with Shafter, however, Miles decided that such action was unnecessary. He confined his moves to ordering the burning of several unsanitary buildings. He was rightly disturbed to learn that Shafter's command had developed what the doctors thought were three cases of yellow fever.

Although the Americans were unaware, the condition of the Spanish troops in Santiago was worse than theirs. General Linares, still in his sickbed, cabled an emotional appeal to Madrid:

> Our troops are exhausted and sickly in an alarming proportion. Cannot be brought to the hospital—needing them in the trenches. Cattle without fodder or hay. Fearful storm of rain, which has been pouring for the past twenty–four hours. Soldiers without permanent shelter. Their only food is rice, and

12. TR letter to Lodge, "Outside Santiago," July 7, 1898. Brands, *Selected Letters of Roosevelt,* 196.
13. Freidel, *The Splendid Little War,* 243.

> not much of that. Our losses were very heavy. Unfortunately, the situation is desperate. The surrender is imminent, otherwise we will only gain time to prolong our agony.
>
> The honor of arms has its limits, and I appeal to the judgment of the Government of the entire Nation, whether these patient troops have not repeatedly saved it since May 18—date of the first bombardment.[14]

The negotiations continued, always coming closer to a Spanish surrender, this time including a surrender of the troops, not just the city. Finally, on July 16, General Toral secured permission to do so. To Shafter's and Miles's astonishment, Toral's surrender offer included the Spanish troops in the entire area—at Guantánamo as well as at Santiago. They were to be returned to Spain in American ships. The terms were signed by commissioners from both sides on that afternoon. Noticeably, nobody from Admiral Sampson's staff was included in the signing party; Sampson and Shafter were indulging in a petty quarrel over the assignment of credit each service should give the other in their respective reports. It is possible that that fact had a bearing.

That unfortunate childishness aside, the overall news was good. General Wheeler, ever dramatic, made his announcement at religious services: "I am pleased to say that there will be no more fighting; the enemy has surrendered."[15]

The formal surrender ceremonies took place at 9:30 on the morning of July 17, 1898. General Shafter and General Toral, each with an escort of a hundred men, met in Santiago and confirmed the agreement. The American flag was raised over the Santiago palace at noon, and during the afternoon successive units of the Spanish Army marched up to San Juan Hill to deposit their arms.[16] They then proceeded to various assigned detention camps, leaving more than two thousand of their comrades in the hospital for wounds or disease. It was now Shafter's responsibility to care for them. Fortunately, Clara Barton and her American Red Cross were still on the scene with the Red Cross ship *The City of Texas.*[17]

The capitulation represented the virtual end of the Spanish–American War. Nelson Miles's later expedition to Puerto Rico was an anticlimax. In the Philippines, the important action for the US Army was not the easy defeat of the Spaniards in Manila Bay, but the slow and bloody subsequent subjugation

14. Ibid., 252.

15. Ibid., 255.

16. Trask, *War with Spain in 1898,* 318, lists these arms as sixteen thousand rifles and three million rounds of ammunition.

17. Ibid., 318.

of the Filipino *insurrectos* themselves, people who expected to become independent upon the removal of the Spaniards.

And what did all this mean to the doughty duo of Theodore Roosevelt and Leonard Wood? Both men had performed with distinction, and both were rewarded handsomely. Roosevelt, aided by Richard Harding Davis and other newsmen, achieved the national reputation he craved, which would later lead to the presidency. And Wood, though overshadowed in the public mind by Roosevelt, was also fortunate. Earlier in the same year of 1898, he had been a captain, Medical Corps, US Army. He was now a brigadier general. Two days after the surrender of Santiago, Wood was appointed military governor of the city, soon to become a brigadier general, not of volunteers, but of the Regular Army.

9

Governor Wood

Leonard Wood's appointment as governor of Santiago removed him from Shafter's force, thereby ending his day–to–day official relationship with Roosevelt. Nevertheless, the friendship and periodic alliances between the two men persisted for the rest of their lives. Before their complete separation, however, they shared in one final significant episode, the so–called round–robin affair. It was no small matter; the fate of the entire Fifth Corps was at stake.

It was obvious to all that the health of Shafter's men was not good, and fear that it would worsen played a large part in Shafter's anxiety to bring the campaign quickly to a close. Once peace was ensured, the matter of health took first priority. The answer was to get the men home. In Roosevelt's estimation, probably derived from Wood, a continued occupation of the Santiago area would cause the death or permanent invalidism of three–quarters of the command.[1]

Still, Secretary of War Alger and presumably President McKinley appeared oblivious to the situation. Shafter's repeated entreaties for relief were refused. In desperation, therefore, Shafter called a council of his general officers to discuss the problem. Wood, as a brigade commander, was of course included, and Roosevelt was unexpectedly invited also, supposedly on the basis that he was the acting commander of a brigade. He soon learned the real reason.

Having given up pleading with Washington, Shafter was contemplating exerting pressure through the press. But because speaking his piece to the reporters in person would be seen as insubordination on his part, he hoped

1. Roosevelt, *An Autobiography,* 245.

to employ a surrogate, more specifically Roosevelt, who was the only officer who enjoyed any prestige with the reporters. Roosevelt was no stranger to controversy, and he held Secretary Alger in no awe, so he impetuously agreed. The others—Kent, Bates, Chaffee, Sumner, Ludlow, Ames, and Wood—were perhaps not surprised by his willingness, but they left the meeting with the understanding that Roosevelt would meet with the members of the press and make them aware of the dangers the command was facing.

Wood, however, held serious doubts about his friend's taking quite so much of the onus on his own shoulders. After the meeting, therefore, he took Roosevelt aside and urged him to pass up the press conference and instead write a letter to Shafter in his capacity as an acting brigade commander. Shafter, Wood argued, could then make the letter public if he chose to, citing Roosevelt as the source. So sold on this idea was Wood that he offered to draft the letter himself. Roosevelt understood and heeded his advice.

Once the letter was written, Roosevelt, in the presence of a group, presented it personally to Shafter, who unexpectedly refused to accept it. A minor scene occurred, in which the paper was shoved around on Shafter's desk. Certain general officers were also present, and they concluded that it was up to them to take collective action. Using Roosevelt's letter as a basis, they signed a round–robin, urging the removal of Fifth Corps from Cuba and its transfer to someplace in the northern part of the United States. That letter Shafter was willing to sign.

In the meantime, however, a draft of Roosevelt's letter leaked to the press in general and appeared in the newspapers even before Alger received it.[2] He and President McKinley were understandably furious at receiving a communication in this fashion, but angry or not, they soon sent orders removing Shafter's command from Cuba in mid–August. The entire force was to be reassembled at Montauk, New York, where the men would be isolated for a time to protect the civilian population from the various tropical diseases they carried.[3]

The new assignment Brigadier General Leonard Wood faced in Santiago turned out to be a critical juncture in his career. Previous to this appointment, his qualities as a soldier and physician had been recognized, but his reputation outside the Army had been limited. He had been overshadowed

2. Ibid., 246–47.

3. The above account comes from Roosevelt's autobiography. Hagedorn, *Leonard Wood, a Biography,* 1:201, makes no mention of Roosevelt.

in the public mind by Theodore Roosevelt. *Wood's Weary Walkers* lacked the panache of the term *Rough Riders.* But as governor of the city of Santiago, his genius for administration and leadership was brought forth in a bright light.

He was taking over a hellhole. To the troops encamped in the mud and rain on the hills around Santiago, the sight of the town gave the false appearance of a haven from the hardships they were enduring. The white stucco walls visible to the troops from a distance promised food, shelter, and excitement. When Wood rode into town, however, he encountered a different sight. As he wrote his wife, "Long lines of wan, yellow, ghastly–looking individuals dragged themselves wearily up and down the filthy streets, avoiding the dead animals and heaps of decomposing refuse, or sank wearily in some friendly shade, seeking to recover strength in sleep. Frightful odors poured out of abandoned houses, speaking more strongly than words of the dead within. The very air seemed laden with death."[4]

Another writer explained the reason for the lack of sanitation as a weird concept on the part of many residents that disease came about not by lack of cleanliness but as an act of God's will. They habitually drank impure water and did little to dispose of personal waste. They habitually stopped by the roadside to relieve themselves and emptied their chamber pots out of windows. As in other less developed parts of the world, Americans were warned, especially if they were out–of–doors during an evening, that they should walk only in the middle of the street and carry an umbrella.

Although certain aspects of this problem may seem amusing to the casual reader, there was nothing light about the gargantuan task that Wood confronted as he occupied the office next to Shafter's in the palace, but he showed no outward concern. In his typical calm, organized fashion, he analyzed the priority of the tasks he faced. First and foremost was the problem of hunger. The city, which in normal times consisted of fifty thousand people, had recently doubled in size, and starvation was prevalent. To meet this condition, Wood immediately set up various food–distribution depots, where he could issue rations, averaging about twenty thousand a day. He wrote home, describing the "long, struggling lines of human beings, tattered and starving, some barely able to stand, others still strong, swayed and pushed and fought fiercely for their places in the line."

Unlike most famines, the victims were not only the poor; all classes and all ages suffered. In his letter, Wood commended the "issue force" that worked from early in the morning until late after dark keeping order. The soldiers

4. Ibid., 184–85.

were sympathetic enough to use their rifles only as bars to keep order and protect the weak. Wood concluded, "These were strange and very unusual sights for an American, and very unpleasant ones. Thousands of people dying with hunger and forgetful of everything else presents a phase of human character not often seen on this side of the world."[5]

Still, it was impossible to save everyone; every day an estimated two hundred people died. Because some of them died alone, Wood's men ignored Spanish and Cuban pleas for privacy and searched the houses. Such corpses as could not be identified were unceremoniously piled into carts and hauled to the outskirts of the city to be burned. There they were piled on gratings of railroad iron and mixed with grass and sticks, soaked with thousands of gallons of kerosene, and soon reduced to ashes. It was the only thing to be done, Wood felt, for the dead threatened the living. He had to avoid a plague.

Along with this disagreeable chore came minor troubles with the Cuban populace. Hardship had not ennobled them. In one instance, when the supply of kerosene ran low, local merchants began running up the price to a Spanish dollar per gallon. Wood called in a group of them and spoke bluntly. The Americans had come to free Cuba, he told them, and they were trying to profit from the sufferings of their countrymen. "You are queer patriots and have a queer way of showing your gratitude. I call such conduct murder." The merchants offered no protests, and the price of kerosene dropped back to normal.[6]

Fortunately, Wood's problems regarding sanitation were greatly eased by the mysterious arrival of a man named George M. Barbour, who termed himself a "sanitary engineer." Although the stranger claimed the title of "major," he was obviously not a regular officer. Nobody, in fact, could learn much about him because his stories were too much to believe. (He claimed, for example, to have once been a partner of Buffalo Bill Cody.) But Wood, a practical man, quickly recognized Barbour's abilities and issued him a major's uniform and appointed him "director of sanitation."

Barbour produced results. He commandeered carts and drafted laborers. He used brutal methods, sometimes resorting to horsewhipping to enforce his orders. He organized his sanitary crews in a military fashion; he even required workers to salute the crew foremen. His workers cleaned shops, bakeries, and slaughterhouses. He cleaned the streets of corpses, removing an estimated eleven hundred bodies, human and animal, in a little more than two months. People using the thoroughfares as sewers were publicly whipped

5. Ibid., 187.
6. Ibid., 188–89.

in the streets of Santiago, and the prominence of an individual was no protection against such treatment. So effective was Barbour's effort, under Wood, of course, that by the middle of the summer of 1899, Wood proclaimed, "The old town is at last clean, and we are down, so to speak, to modern dirt which, while not attractive, is of a less offensive character than that of 1520."[7]

It was well that Wood had Barbour to assist him, because early in the game he himself came down with a sickness he called malaria, but which he privately diagnosed as yellow fever. But despite his fever and sickness, Wood remained on duty, riding around the city twice a day to inspect the progress of the cleanup.

While Wood was cleaning up the city of Santiago and feeding the people, the matter of jurisdiction remained in doubt. The Spanish garrison had surrendered to the Americans, and the American flag had been raised over the palace, but at a higher level of government things were not so easy. Because no peace treaty had been signed between the United States and Spain, the island—or at least those parts not occupied by American troops—technically remained Spanish. In addition, Shafter's mission, to assist in destroying Cervera's fleet, had been accomplished, leaving little reason for a continued occupation. To complicate matters, Garcia's Cuban rebels believed that they should be in charge. As an interim measure, therefore, the Americans simply enforced the status quo until Fifth Corps departed for Montauk in the middle of August. At that time, Shafter left five thousand American troops under the command of General Lawton, naming him the governor of Santiago Province. Wood was once more Lawton's subordinate, though Lawton granted him a great deal of latitude.

To the Cubans in the streets, however, other concerns remained. The Spanish surrender of authority in Santiago did not mean that the former colonists themselves had left; they had simply remained in their homes. Understandably, they were now in danger; the Cubans remembered the high-handed and sometimes cruel Spanish government. But for the moment, Wood maintained things as they were. When he learned that two young Cubans intended to establish a newspaper advocating "Santiago for the Cubans," he refused permission. He would guarantee the rights of Spanish as well as Cubans. The two young men left a conference with him in a huff, but the newspaper was never established.[8]

7. The year 1520 was that in which the town of Santiago had been founded.
8. Ibid., 203.

One evening in late September, Wood made one concession. He permitted the Cubans to hold a celebration of the Spanish downfall. Unfortunately, the participants came under the influence of too much liquor, the festivities degenerated into a tumult, and the mob began to throw stones at the San Carlos Club, a Spanish gathering place. A threat of physical violence arose. Wood, who was still in his nearby office, heard of the crisis. He took a sentry to the club, carrying only his customary riding crop. He gave the sentry an order: "Shoot the first man who places his foot on that step." The mob dispersed, and Wood returned to his desk.[9]

As time went on, armed bands of former Cuban rebels began demobilizing, dispersing from their former units and heading home. The presence of idle ex–soldiers on the streets of Santiago posed a threat. Wood therefore put them to work. There was plenty of work to do. Fortunately, the departure of Spanish officials had left many administrative jobs open, and many unemployed former rebels were able to fill them. Further, Wood needed laborers to reconstruct the worn–down infrastructure. The roads, in particular, were in miserable condition, and Wood resolved not just to restore them but to pave them. Doing so would cost twenty–five thousand dollars, about 3 percent of the price the corrupt Spanish government had charged. But here Wood ran into a new problem in the person of his friend and boss, Henry Lawton.

Lawton, as an old–line regular, had little taste for such mundane matters as administration and cleaning up. Up to this point, he had allowed Wood to take care of such things, especially in the city. But when Wood approached him with a bill he considered exorbitant, he balked. Wood somehow wheedled his funds but at the price of offending his old friend.

They never completely made up. The friction between them was solved in a manner that Wood could not like. Lawton, an occasional binge drinker, went on a spree that could not be concealed, despite the efforts of his aides. Ordinarily, the Old Army was able to protect such "twenty–eight–day soldiers," for it had many members who habitually gave the Army their all for a month but then went out of action on payday. Such conduct, however, was not expected of the governor of Santiago Province, especially because Lawton's binge continued for several days, in which he caused damage to property. When word of the episode got back to Washington, Lawton was relieved and Wood was appointed governor of Santiago Province in his place.

It was here that the chronic resentment of Wood's unconventional rise to high position found a chink in his armor. Many regulars, especially West

9. Ibid., 205.

Pointers, began a whispering campaign that accused Wood of leaking the word of Lawton's misdemeanor to his friends in Washington. So far as is known, Wood was innocent, but the suspicion of his alleged disloyalty followed him the rest of his life.

A more serious mishap took place at about the time that Wood took over the position as governor; he suffered a severe accident to his head. He was able to brush it off at the time, but the symptoms grew with the years and eventually caused his death. As Wood himself described it, "My desk was in a particular room of the house there, and I got accustomed to the location. One very warm day my secretary moved the desk to another room where there was a chance of getting more air. Someone called me and I got up suddenly. Directly behind me there was a hanging chandelier. It must have been hanging extremely low for when I arose my head came in violent contact with it. The blow must have broken my skull."

Broken skull or not, Wood was not immediately disabled. After falling to the floor, he regained his feet, washed the wound, and went back to work until the pain forced him to stop. Nevertheless, despite a lump the size of his fist, Wood was back at work the next day and the lump gradually diminished.[10]

Wood did a competent and dedicated job both at Santiago City and in Santiago Province. Unfortunately, however, his activities were not above reproach, for he was also accused of being overly concerned with promoting his own personal interests. Like Roosevelt he was an ambitious man, and also like Roosevelt he tended to disregard the means by which he obtained his ends. Thus, as governor of Santiago Province, he developed an ambition to replace Major General John R. Brooke as governor–general of all of Cuba, in Havana. Roosevelt helped wholeheartedly.

Wood and Roosevelt's two–man cabal—for that is what it was—succeeded because they knew exactly what they wanted. Besides Wood's elevation to be governor–general of Cuba, they were also convinced that the United States should annex the island permanently, regardless of the Teller Amendment to the US declaration of war against Spain. They also desired to rebuild Cuba. Whereas McKinley and Brooke were content with merely removing the Spanish from Cuba, Wood and Roosevelt were convinced that Cubans, as inferior beings, would not be able to govern themselves. Their objective was to "Americanize" the island as much as possible.

10. Ibid., 210–11.

The endeavors were far from subtle. Wood, for example, did his best to convince the new secretary of war, Elihu Root, that he, Wood, as governor of Santiago Province, should report directly to the secretary rather than through Brooke.[11] He also attempted to attain authority for customs revenues collected at the port of Santiago to be used for the benefit of Santiago Province alone rather than sent to Havana for the general welfare. Root refused to accept either of Wood's outlandish schemes, but the fact that Wood possessed the temerity to try illustrates the degree of disagreement between him and Brooke.

Root finally gave in. Although Brooke's attitude toward Cuba was closer to McKinley's thinking than it was to that of Wood, Root on his own had concluded that Brooke was not the man to govern Cuba. At age sixty, a veteran of the Civil War, he lacked the energy to perform all the functions the job required. McKinley and Root therefore set about to find a replacement. Because a familiarity with Cuban problems was an important qualification for the job of governor, they decided to choose from the governors of the four provinces.[12] All four were seeking the governorship, but all went about promoting their cases in different ways. General James H. Wilson, for example, presented a plan for Cuba's future that was ultimately accepted nearly in its entirety, though not Wilson himself. Wood used the political route. He secured permission to visit Washington, where he was hailed as the last surviving hero of the Cuban campaign still on active duty. He was feted and granted permission to visit New York and Washington. He had an audience with McKinley. An enraged Brooke, in Havana, attempted to prevent Wood's politicking, but to no avail.

Wilson may have been a better–qualified candidate for the position of governor than Wood, but with Roosevelt's backing, Wood commanded the firepower. Roosevelt, on his own volition, showed Root one of Wood's letters excoriating Brooke. Root could not have admired that disloyalty, but he was a practical man, so he gave in to the pressure. On December 13, 1899, President William McKinley announced the appointment of Leonard Wood, now a brigadier general in the Regular Army, to be the governor–general of Cuba. The Wood–Roosevelt team had triumphed once more.

Although Wood's tactics in securing the governorship of all of Cuba were questionable, there is no doubt that he was eminently qualified for the posi-

11. For more on Root, see the next chapter.

12. Matanza and Santa Clara, commanded by Wilson; the Department of Havana and the Province of Pinar de Rio, commanded by Fitzhugh Lee; the Department of Havana, commanded by William S. Ludlow; and the Department of Santiago, commanded by Wood.

tion. His medical background and his experience in Santiago Province had prepared him well. He put the administrative affairs in order and reestablished the educational, police, and fiscal systems. He modernized the justice system and brought about an understanding between church and state in a country in which the two had previously been solidified under Spain. He encouraged agriculture and commerce. Appropriately, it was under Wood's administration as governor that Major Walter Reed, Army Medical Corps, made his pivotal research into the causes and prevention of yellow fever, an accomplishment that later made construction of the Panama Canal possible.

But Wood's was also an authoritarian regime, and he tolerated no slurs on the part of Cubans against the occupying Americans. A Cuban newspaper, *La Discusion*, carried a cartoon showing the Cuban people as Christ on the cross with Leonard Wood and William McKinley as the other two thieves. Wood forthwith had the owner of the newspaper, one Dr. Manuel Coronado, and the cartoonist, Jesus Castellanos, incarcerated.

Oddly, the episode that caused Wood difficulties in later years involved not a Cuban but an American. During the American occupation, the Cuban postal service operated under American auspices, and the position of director was considered something of a political plum. The director, Estes R. Rathbone, had friends in Washington, a product of patronage. It was something of a shock, therefore, when word of corruption on his part reached Wood. He launched an investigation, which turned up that Rathbone had been enriching himself handsomely at the public expense. A full 10 percent of the revenues of the postal system, it was found, had wound up in Rathbone's pockets.

Wood took immediate action. He removed Rathbone and incarcerated him. Rathbone retaliated by applying for a congressional investigation of his actions, backed up by Mark Hanna, the super–fund–raiser for President McKinley and the enemy of Theodore Roosevelt. Knowing of the close friendship between Roosevelt and Wood, Hanna put Wood on his own enemies list. Wood always regarded the Rathbone episode as the greatest blot on his administration of Cuba. Granted, he had taken firm action against corruption. The reason he blamed himself was for failing to catch up with Rathbone's activities before he actually had.[13]

Cuba was declared an independent country in May 1902, and on the twentieth day of that month Wood's tenure as governor ceased. He returned to the United States for a short while and visited Europe, conversing at least briefly with Kaiser Wilhelm II of Germany. That period over, he was available for whatever duty President Roosevelt desired.

13. Jack C. Lane, *Armed Progressive: General Leonard Wood*, 97.

10

Tom Platt Creates a President

Alger and McKinley were rightfully angry to learn of Shafter's "round–robin," especially since it reached them by way of the newspapers. To boot, they somehow learned of Roosevelt's role in giving it impetus.[1] Nevertheless, in public they reacted cautiously, confining their actions to writing a letter of rebuke to Roosevelt. And despite the violation of procedure, they saw the light or felt the heat and lost no time in implementing the recommendations. On August 5, 1898, McKinley issued an order designating an area near Montauk, New York, as a place for Fifth Corps to assemble, pending the dispersal of the regulars and the demobilization of the volunteers. The location had been chosen because it afforded a healthy spot far enough away from population centers to make a quarantine meaningful. It was named after Colonel Charles A. Wikoff, commander of the 3d Brigade, 1st Division, killed at San Juan Hill.

Two days later, on August 7, 1898, the remnants of the Rough Riders and two troops of regular cavalry, under the command of Wheeler and Roosevelt, sailed from Cuba, headed for home. Nine days later, they arrived at Fort Long Bay, near Montauk.

The reception they received presaged things to come. Despite Wheeler's position as the commander, all eyes were focused on his subordinate, Roosevelt. The 1st Volunteer Cavalry was proclaimed to be America's favorite regiment, and Roosevelt was already being mentioned as a possible Republican candidate for governor of New York. Roosevelt basked in the attention, but

1. For Roosevelt's letter to Shafter and the separate round–robin, see Jeff Heatley, ed., *Bully! Colonel Theodore Roosevelt, the Rough Riders, and Camp Wikoff, Montauk, New York, 1898*, 13–15.

he was shrewd enough to avoid all talk of politics—or tried to. While emphasizing the bravery of his men and his concern for them, he exhibited no false modesty. To a reporter's question as to his health, he answered, "I am feeling disgracefully well. . . . I feel positively ashamed of my appearance when I see how badly off some of my brave fellows are—Oh, but we have had a bully fight!" This was his men's hour, he insisted; politics could wait.[2] Roosevelt went to Camp Wikoff with his Rough Riders.

The new hero did not delay, however, in plunging into politics. Even while he and his men were undergoing their obligatory five days of quarantine, he sent a message to Representative Lemuel Quigg, an old friend and the titular head of the Republican Party in New York. "CAN YOU GET HERE TOMORROW OR FRIDAY? CAN PUT YOU UP FOR THE NIGHT. WOULD PARTICULARLY LIKE TO TALK OVER MATTERS WITH YOU."[3] Quigg had every right to be offended by such a peremptory demand coming from a colonel of volunteer cavalry, but he, like everyone else, was conscious that Roosevelt was the man of the hour, possibly the most popular man in the country. So Quigg cheerfully turned up as he was bidden.

Quigg's alacrity in meeting Roosevelt's bidding can be attributed to the fact that he had an agenda of his own: he came as the agent of Senator Thomas Platt, who despite Quigg's title was the undisputed boss of New York Republican politics. Platt was using Quigg to feel out Roosevelt's intentions concerning the upcoming race for governor. Roosevelt answered enthusiastically: he would run. In response, Quigg volunteered his own opinion that Platt, who controlled some seventy out of the approximately one hundred delegates, would support him. But he, Quigg, emphasized that he was not authorized to commit Platt in any way.[4]

Roosevelt stayed at Camp Wikoff until the Rough Riders were disbanded on August 20, but his mind had moved on. During his time in camp, he received numerous visitors, mostly political operatives. When he and his wife, Edith, arrived back at Oyster Bay, they were met by a rousing, almost frenzied, reception. But despite his popularity, he was still the supplicant. The next day, he called on Platt himself, at the senator's Fifth Avenue hotel in Manhattan.

Thomas Collier Platt, known as the "Easy Boss" for his quiet and courteous demeanor, looked much older than his fifty-eight years—thin and stooped.

2. Brands, *T. R.,* 363. See also Heatley, *Bully!,* 63.
3. Thomas, *The War Lovers,* 359.
4. Roosevelt, *An Autobiography,* 271.

But he dressed meticulously, and his quiet manner fooled nobody; he was recognized as tough and ruthless. Platt's sole criterion in judging a prospective candidate for office was how that man, once elected, could be used to maintain his own, Platt's, power. For that reason, Platt was dubious about Roosevelt's candidacy. In public, however, he had to cope with great pressures to appear favorable. His problem was reinforced by the fact that the incumbent Republican governor, Frank Black, was considered a political liability because of a scandal regarding the financing of repairs on the Erie Canal. Finally, even Platt was dependent on the financial backing of New York industry, who favored Roosevelt. So when queried, Platt expressed his support for Roosevelt, though his wording was a model of obfuscation: "If Colonel Roosevelt is nominated, we have nominated for governor a man who has demonstrated in public office and on the battlefield that he is a fighter for the right, and always victorious. If he is elected, you know and we all know from his demonstrated characteristics, courage and ability, that every thief will be caught and punished and every dollar that can be found restored to the public treasury. Then I will follow the colonel leading his Rough Riders up San Juan Hill and ask the band to play the Star Spangled Banner."[5]

Despite Platt's reservations about Roosevelt, he hid them well, even from Roosevelt himself. After the meeting, therefore, Roosevelt was certain of the boss's support. He wrote to Lodge, "Apparently I am going to be nominated. I saw Platt the other day, and had an entirely satisfactory talk. Of course I shall have great trouble in the governorship, but there is no use shirking responsibilities."[6]

The two men were not meeting for the first time. They had a long, mixed relationship stretching over the years. Platt had once, in fact, attempted to remove Roosevelt as New York police commissioner. Based on that history, Platt was doubly suspicious about the independence Roosevelt might exercise as governor. But Platt's advisers and mainstays were adamant. After the loudly touted sins of Governor Black, the only Republican who could save New York from going Democratic in the fall election was Roosevelt. Accordingly, Platt virtually handed Roosevelt the Republican gubernatorial nomination in September 1898.

If there was one matter that interested Roosevelt more than attaining the governorship of New York, it was his lust to receive the Congressional Medal of Honor for his actions on San Juan Hill. He had sought and obtained rec-

5. Brands, *T. R.*, 364.
6. Roosevelt to Lodge, September 19, 1898. Brands, *Selected Letters of Roosevelt*, 211.

ommendations for the nation's highest decoration from Wood, Wheeler, and a somewhat reluctant Shafter. His candidacy for the honor was touted by both Richard Harding Davis and Stephen Crane. But he was justifiably suspicious that Secretary of War Alger and President McKinley had their doubts about awarding him the medal. Perhaps influenced by the views of such regulars as John J. Pershing, who had not been impressed by the Rough Riders on that July 1, Alger took no action. Roosevelt, shedding all inhibitions and niceties, wrote to various officials, and he was blunt. In a letter to Lodge, for example, whimsically writing about his own eventual demise, he appended, "And, old man, if I do go, I do wish you would get that Medal of Honor for me anyhow, as I should awfully like the children to have it, and I think I earned it."[7]

It was no use. Both Secretary Alger and President McKinley remained unconvinced. Eventually, Roosevelt gave up.

Although Platt's backing made Roosevelt's nomination for the governorship of New York State essentially ensured, an unexpected hurdle appeared when a supporter of Governor Black questioned Roosevelt's status as a citizen of New York. He had been away a long time and had not paid taxes in the state for years. To fight his case, Roosevelt hired a prominent lawyer from New York City named Elihu Root. Root looked at the case and found a roundabout way to beat the allegation. But Roosevelt was shaken by the episode and at one point mentioned to Platt that he might withdraw his name. Platt, whose mind was by now made up, understood his candidate's psychology. "Is the hero of San Juan Hill a coward?" he asked. "By God! I'll run." That ended the problem.[8]

The electoral campaign concentrated largely on personalities, featuring the matter of corruption. The Democratic candidate, Augustus Van Wyk, was a handpicked candidate of Tammany Hall, and enough corruption existed in that organization to provide plenty of ammunition for Roosevelt. The record of Governor Black, a Republican, provided the same fodder for Van Wyk. As always, Roosevelt made full use of the aura he had gained in Cuba. He took a bugler along with him on the campaign trail, along with several wounded veterans of the Rough Riders. That seemed to be a good idea, but the men he took with him were too unsophisticated to discern between what a soldier might admire and what a voter might consider appropriate.[9]

7. Morris, *Rise of Theodore Roosevelt,* 661.

8. Ibid., 678.

9. One soldier made a statement that could not have helped. "My friends and fellow citizens, my colonel was a great soldier. He will make a great governor. He always put us boys in battle where we would be killed if there was a chance, and that is what he will do with you." Brands, *T. R.,* 367.

Roosevelt's campaign manager quickly dispensed with the services of Roosevelt's Rough Riders.

When election day rolled around, the vote was extremely close. Out of a total of 1.3 million registered voters, the hero of San Juan Hill won by fewer than 18,000.[10]

Trouble between Roosevelt and Platt broke out as soon as the election was decided, in fact even before TR's inauguration. It soon became apparent that despite Platt's intention to retain power in his own hands, Roosevelt intended to be his own man. A favorite friend and supporter of Platt's, seeking appointment to a certain post on the Erie Canal, made his application to Senator Platt, as was the custom. Platt promised the man the position and mentioned the matter to Roosevelt almost in passing. An angry Roosevelt overruled him; the man had a conflict of interest, he contended, because he owned property along the canal. Platt exploded, but he finally realized that he had no recourse and gave in. And although the two men maintained an outward friendship, holding meetings weekly in New York, it was obvious that Roosevelt was a threat to Platt's position.

Roosevelt went even further. Backed by the support of Platt's enemies, he took other measures as governor that made him unpalatable to the Easy Boss. But despite the fracases, the governor did not find the job of governor overly taxing. The legislature did not sit in session all year long, so when it closed in early 1899, he wrote to Lodge, saying with relief that the heavy work, so far as he was concerned, was over for 1899.[11] The position thus allowed him time to engage in his writing, which he still at least partway considered his primary profession. While in office, he wrote a biography of Oliver Cromwell. By and large, he liked his present position and might well have run for a second two–year term. But it was not to be.

Roosevelt may have been governor of New York, a war hero, and possibly the most popular man in the country, but he could not name his successor as governor; Tom Platt was still the boss of the New York State Republican Party. And Platt had come to the conclusion that New York did not have room for both him and Roosevelt. He therefore resolved to get Roosevelt out of office. From a political viewpoint, of course, it would be best to attain his end without a direct confrontation. After some thought, he came up with a way of handling the problem. Knowing that the Republicans, in-

10. Ibid., 368.
11. Brands, *Selected Letters of Roosevelt,* 219.

cluding McKinley, were dissatisfied with the incumbent vice president, Platt began touting Roosevelt for that position. Roosevelt had some idea of what was going on. In early–February 1900, he wrote to his habitual correspondent, Lodge, "Have found out one reason why Senator Platt wants me nominated for the Vice–Presidency. He is, I am convinced, genuinely friendly, and indeed I may say really fond of me, and is perfectly satisfied with the way I have conducted politics, but the big–moneyed men with whom he is in close touch and whose campaign contributions have certainly been no inconsiderable factor in his strength, have been pressing him very strongly to get me put in the Vice–Presidency."[12]

Roosevelt had the situation figured right, and he was far from happy with the prospect. The office of vice president at the turn of the twentieth century was not a desirable one. The vice president was not considered to be a member of the presidential administration, and his constitutional duty of presiding over the Senate, deprived of a voice of his own, was not something that a man of Roosevelt's vociferous nature would enjoy. Moreover, he resented Platt's activities. Therefore, when Platt informed him that he would not be renominated for governor, Roosevelt replied heatedly. He declared that he would accept Platt's challenge and would remove his name from the list of vice presidential possibilities. He would defy Platt and run for governor.

When Roosevelt's intentions became known nationally, however, the decision transcended New York politics. The Republican delegations from other states, realizing how important the Roosevelt name would be to the Republican ticket, now raised their voices in his support. As a good party man, Roosevelt decided to accept the nomination, thus producing the McKinley–Roosevelt Republican ticket.[13]

But Theodore Roosevelt could never take a backseat, even to the president. He attended the Republican Convention of 1900 wearing a Rough Rider's hat and a red bandanna.

The McKinley–Roosevelt ticket won handily over William Jennings Bryan and Adlai Stevenson in the presidential election, and Roosevelt fell into a period of mixed emotions. He harbored a burning ambition to be president, but at that time the vice presidency was not considered to be a stepping–stone to the presidency. Not since Martin Van Buren was elected president in 1836 had a sitting vice president succeeded his former boss. And to rise to the presidency by virtue of the death of the president was something for which a civilized

12. Ibid., 237–38.
13. Roosevelt, *An Autobiography,* 300.

man could never hope. So Roosevelt performed his duties, remembered with fondness the hoopla of the 1900 campaign, and kept his mouth shut.

Six months after the McKinley–Roosevelt inauguration, all that changed. On September 6, 1901, President McKinley was shot as he and his wife were attending the Pan–American Exposition in Buffalo, New York. An anarchist by the name of Leon Czolgosz stepped up, aimed a pistol, and pumped two bullets into the belly of the president. McKinley was rushed to the hospital, where the doctors found that a bullet had passed through his body, tearing the stomach in front and back. The prognosis was questionable.

At the time of this incident, Roosevelt was on a speaking tour in Vermont. His immediate reaction, as he later claimed to Lodge, was "stunned amazement," but his feelings ranged from one thought to another, depending on his moods.[14] He was discreet about his own future, and in his letters, at least, he focused on railing against anarchists, not only Czolgosz but all others. He went even further, condemning those people such as Hearst, who played upon the violent side of human emotions. He castigated all those who sympathized in any degree with anarchists, including such unlikely persons as Russian novelist Leo Tolstoy. Perhaps Roosevelt's days as police commissioner in New York had affected him, for despite his own maverick ways he was almost obsessed with hatred of anarchists.

Despite those emotions, expressed privately to Lodge, Roosevelt was facing a very practical question: what should he do while the crisis was pending? After all, he was no ordinary citizen; he was heir to the presidency. And for the moment, he was only McKinley's vice president. He did not ponder long, however. He commandeered a train and rushed to Buffalo, where he learned that McKinley showed every sign of a full recovery. Day by day, Roosevelt's letters to friends became more and more optimistic regarding the president's condition. By September 10, three days after his arrival at Buffalo, Roosevelt felt it safe to leave. He joined Edith and their children where they were vacationing at a resort called Tahawus in the Adirondacks.

Confident that McKinley's recovery was ensured, Roosevelt made plans for a little exercise. He chose to climb a hill named Mount Marcy, an easy task, but Edith was cautious. Aware of Roosevelt's tendency to wander out of the reach of civilization, she insisted that she and the children go along, and the party soon expanded.

They left in the rain at noontime on September 12 and by the end of the day's climb had reached a point not quite at the summit. There they encamp-

14. Brands, *T. R.*, 411.

ed for the night, and the next morning, the thirteenth, Roosevelt and a guide continued in the rain and clouds to the top, while Edith and the rest returned to Tahawus. Roosevelt reached the crest of Mount Marcy by noon and then, with visibility zero, with rain and cold, they descended a short way down the hill and broke out their lunches.

Hardly had Roosevelt begun eating when he spied a messenger trudging up the trail. As Roosevelt later claimed, he could tell at a glance that the man bore bad news. It was a dispatch from President McKinley's personal secretary, with somber words: "The President's condition has changed for the worse."[15] Without finishing lunch, Roosevelt packed up and headed back down to Tahawus. The trail was wet and slippery, so it was late in the afternoon when he arrived. Then, since no further messages had arrived, Roosevelt and his family had dinner and went to bed.

They had only two hours to sleep. A second messenger arrived at the door with word that the president was slipping fast and that the end of his life was near. Roosevelt's duty was now clear; his place was in Buffalo. He slipped on his clothes and called for a driver and a cart. The trip down the mountain to the railroad at North Creek was a harrowing one, and only the fact that the driver and his horses knew the territory made it possible for them to make the trip. As it was, the two men had to make stops to change horse teams twice. It was dawn before an exhausted, sleepless Roosevelt arrived at North Creek, where a train waited to take him on the four–hour trip to Buffalo. At that very moment, unbeknownst to Roosevelt, President McKinley died. Roosevelt was president as of September 14, 1901.

Roosevelt's duties were now plain. He was taken to the house where McKinley's body lay. He paid his condolences to the McKinley family and reassured the country that the policies of his predecessor would be continued. He was then sworn into office by a local justice of the peace.

Theodore Roosevelt was now president of the United States. He was not proud of the indirect way by which he had come by this position of honor, but there was little time to ponder. He had work to do.

Tom Platt had engineered Roosevelt's departure from New York. Making his political associate president was not, however, exactly what Platt had had in mind.

15. Ibid., 141.

11

Commander in Chief

A president of the United States plays many roles—chief of state, chief executive, party leader, moral leader, among others. But the role that seems to give the greatest pride to a president is that of commander in chief of the armed forces. Certainly, it was a role that Theodore Roosevelt relished.

By the time Roosevelt assumed the presidency on the death of McKinley, the war between Spain and the United States was long over. Its aftermath, however, the fighting between the Americans and the Philippine *insurrectos,* was still dragging on, though it had been temporarily relegated to the back burner in the minds of the American public. Roosevelt was free to turn his attention to reorganizing the War Department. As one of the most vociferous critics of the Army's mismanagement of the Spanish–American War, he was determined to rectify the worst of the evils that had caused so many needless casualties in that conflict. The effort was already under way. President McKinley had taken the first steps back in 1899 when he removed the congenial but largely ineffective secretary of war, Russell A. Alger. As Alger's successor, McKinley had chosen New York lawyer Elihu Root.

Root, at age fifty–four, had never held public office, but he was a highly respected corporate lawyer. He had, it will be recalled, represented Roosevelt when the latter had needed to establish his New York credentials while campaigning for the governorship in 1898. Root's list of clients was wide; it ranged from former president Chester A. Arthur to William "Boss" Tweed. When McKinley summoned him to be secretary of war, he was serving as US attorney for the Southern District of New York, and he had no desire to leave that position. Among other considerations, he was reluctant to leave New York and move to Washington. But McKinley prevailed on his patriotism, and Root had finally accepted. When Roosevelt succeeded to the presidency on McKinley's death, Root willingly stayed on.

Although McKinley had begun the process, it was Roosevelt who gave impetus to the Army reorganization. Spurred on by the president, Root focused his efforts in that direction. He began by launching a study of existing military systems, both foreign and domestic. Most important to his study was a body of work produced by Brevet Major General Emory Upton, a Civil War hero and the author of several books on military organization. Upton's most meaningful writing was an unfinished manuscript, "The Military Policy of the United States," which Root immediately ordered published as a book. Upton's views could not be taken in full, because they reflected the young officer's distaste for the American concept of civilian control of the military. But it was not philosophy that Root was seeking; it was Upton's studies of organization. And central to all that study was the need to create a general staff, something previously neglected in the United States Army.

Upton's manuscript, begun in 1875, had been much influenced by his personal contacts with the Prussian General Staff, which enjoyed a unique position in German hierarchy. Ever since Field Marshal Helmuth von Moltke of Prussia had directed the decisive defeat of Napoleon III's France in the War of 1870–71, it had been viewed in military circles with something approaching awe.[1] The core of this system lay in its professionalism and the meticulous selection of its members. Its stability had made it into a sort of cult, because its members, if they stayed in favor, remained in the organization for their entire careers. By no means, however, was it an ivory tower. To prevent its members from losing touch with reality, it required every officer to serve periodic tours in the field with troops. It worked well, at least for Germans. The General Staff provided both intelligent guidance and continuity.[2]

Upton had also studied other systems, such as the French, who also employed a form of general staff, but the French version was loose and casual in comparison with the Germans. Its members, for example, were not set aside from their peers, instead being drawn only on a temporary basis from troops in the regular lines. Besides, France's recent defeat by its Teutonic rival had done nothing to enhance its prestige.

1. The word *general* in its name signified that it concerned itself with overall military strategy, not with a single service.

2. In the field, they were given higher rank. But when Captain Erich von Ludendorff was sent to command a unit as a lieutenant colonel, he was reported to have moaned, "My influence plummeted immeasurably."

In studying Upton's works, Root quickly rejected any attempt to establish a body such as the German system in the United States Army. The Americans would never tolerate even the more moderate French system. Root therefore drew on one of Upton's other concepts and created the Army War College. The primary purpose of such a college, of course, would be the broad education of senior officers, but the same organization was also used as a planning group to supplement the small, inadequate staff allowed by Congress, which was limited to fifty–five officers, each restricted to tours no longer than four years.

Besides the inevitable limitations on a general staff imposed by Congress, Root faced another obstacle in reorganizing, to strengthen the authority of the uniformed general in chief over the technical services—engineers, quartermaster, ordnance, and adjutant general. Throughout American history, these fiefdoms had reported directly to the secretary of war, independently of the general in chief. These tech services controlled much patronage in civilian jobs and lucrative contracts and were therefore influential with many members of Congress. The general in chief had no such clout. Root therefore realized that he had to work through Congress; he could not instantly deprive the technical services of their privileged status. He therefore proposed disestablishing the general–in–chief position and creating a new position, "chief of staff"—that is, chief of staff to the secretary of war. Thus, the ranking man in uniform could coordinate all the ancillary functions of the Army, but not on his own authority. He signed orders in the name of the secretary, an arrangement the technical services could not argue with.

Root's plan met resistance from the influential General Nelson A. Miles, who interpreted the reorganization, especially the change of title, as a reduction in his own prestige. Never mind that under Root's reorganization plan, he personally would actually gain power. And though Miles had long been out of favor with the Cleveland and McKinley administrations, he was a force to contend with because of the respect he enjoyed in Congress. His political influence in that body was enhanced by rumors that he, like Admiral George Dewey, was a possible presidential candidate.

But all that was long going; troubles of an acute nature arose soon after Roosevelt took over as president. One was the so–called Sampson–Schley affair, and the other was the question of the US policy toward the Philippines.

The Sampson–Schley controversy was actually a trivial matter that had nothing to do with the Army. A conflict had arisen within the Navy as to who should receive the credit for the American victory over the Spanish at Santiago Bay back on July 3, 1898. Admiral Sampson had been in overall command, but in his absence Commodore Winfield S. Schley had actually fought the battle. So virulent was the dispute that an enraged Schley had demanded a court of inquiry, which was automatically granted. The three–member board, which met in early–November 1901 and was chaired by Admiral George Dewey, voted two to one in favor of Sampson. Dewey himself, however, dissented. His two colleagues, he claimed, were unqualified to judge because they had never commanded ships in combat.[3]

There the matter should have dropped, but for some reason Miles could not resist commenting. On December 17, 1901, he was quoted in the *New York Times* as supporting Dewey's conclusions favoring Schley.[4] The bulk of the American public agreed, probably influenced by universal admiration that the citizenry held for Miles and Dewey.

Miles's statement, however, infuriated Secretary Root. He was unconcerned with the actual merits of the case, but he disapproved of Miles's expressing an opinion, which regulations forbade. When Root sent for Miles, the general readily admitted the facts of the case. He claimed that he was speaking only as a private citizen, not as a general. Root, unconvinced, censured Miles in no uncertain terms: "You had no business in this controversy, and no right, holding the office you did, to express any opinion. Your conduct was in violation of the regulation above cited, and the rules of official propriety, and you are justly liable to censure, which I now express."[5]

Roosevelt had watched the whole debacle, but he had left its handling in Root's hands. By now Roosevelt and Root had lumped Miles with Dewey as two officers with politics in mind. But Root's severe rebuff further damaged the relations between the administration and the proud Nelson Miles.

Root's reprimand of Miles was no more than a mere slap on the wrist compared to the general in chief's differences with the president over the conduct of the continued fighting in the Philippines. That was a matter of import.

By late–September 1901, the fighting in the Philippines seemed to be settling down. Most of the islands had been pacified, and those areas where fighting had ceased were now being administered by a civilian governor, future president William Howard Taft. Those islands where fighting continued were under the control of the Army's Philippine Division, under Major

3. Commodore Schley was the senior officer of the US squadron off Santiago when the Spanish squadron attempted to escape on the morning of July 3, 1898. He was in absolute command and is entitled to the credit due to such a commanding officer for the glorious victory that resulted in the total destruction of the Spanish ships. *New York Times,* December 14, 1901, quoted in Arthur Amchan, *The Most Famous Soldier in America: A Biography of Lt. Gen. Nelson A. Miles, 1839–1925,* 147–48.

4. *New York Times,* December 17, 1901, quoted in ibid., 149.

5. *New York Times,* December 22, 1901, quoted in ibid., 150.

General Adna Chaffee, who enjoyed considerable success in buying off hostile chieftains. The still–hostile area was concentrated in the so–called Southern Islands, and policies were being conducted under the provisions of an antiquated document, General Order 100, which had been issued in 1863 to direct how the Union army should deal with Confederate guerrillas. The crux of that order was to do everything possible to protect friendly civilians but to employ extremely harsh measures over insurgents.[6]

On September 28, 1901, only two weeks after Theodore Roosevelt had assumed office, the tranquillity in the Southern Islands of the Philippines was badly shaken. At the small town of Balangiga, on the island of Samar, insurgent guerrillas raided an Army garrison, leaving forty–eight American soldiers dead. When word of the disaster reached the United States, the public reaction approached hysteria: "the greatest American defeat since the Battle of the Little Big Horn." The local American commander, Brigadier General Jacob Smith, reacted accordingly. In a fit of rage, Smith spoke foolishly to Major Littleton Waller, whose Marine battalion was part of Smith's command. Smith's words were blunt and quotable, implying orders to "kill and burn and make a howling wilderness of Samar."[7] Smith was also reported to have ordered all male citizens in the city above the age of ten to be shot. He put his words into action: he burned crops and blocked off all trade with the adjacent island of Leyte in order to ensure that the insurgents in the hills of Samar were not fed by the people in the towns and adjacent islands.

The fighting on Samar soon came to an end, and the emaciated insurgent leader, Vicente Lukban, surrendered. But in the meantime, the death toll among the native population of Samar had reached a reported two thousand civilians of all ages and genders. General Smith was subsequently court–martialed for his actions and as a result was forced to retire from the Army. It is notable, however, that the bulk of his colleagues thought that he had behaved correctly.[8] The focus had now switched from the deaths of the forty–eight American soldiers onto the brutality of American policy toward the Philippine population.

6. Thomas Bruno, "Samar: The Violent End of Insurgency," 33.

7. Elting E. Morison, ed., *The Letters of Theodore Roosevelt,* 3:256, quoted in Amchan, *Most Famous Soldier in America,* 159.

8. "I personally strung up thirty–five Filipinos without trial, so what was all the fuss over Waller's 'dispatching' a few 'treacherous savages'? If there had been more Smiths and Wallers, the war would have been over long ago. Impromptu domestic hanging might also hasten the end of the war. For starters, all Americans who had recently petitioned Congress to sue for peace in the Philippines should be dragged out of their homes and lynched." General Frederick Funston, *New York Sun,* March 10, 1902, cited in Stuart Creighton Miller, *Benevolent Assimilation: The American Conquest of the Philippines, 1899–1903,* 234–35.

The episode had an odd repercussion. An unrepentant General Miles saw the tragedy as an opportunity for himself. He presented a memo to Root, declaring that the situation in the Philippines was being handled "with marked severity," and to rectify the situation he suggested that he personally should be sent to Manila to replace both Governor–General Taft and General Chaffee. Predictably, his preposterous letter leaked to the press, thereby putting the president on the spot.

Miles's proposal to take charge in Manila was easily dismissed, but what infuriated Roosevelt and Root was that, in describing the Philippine situation, Miles had refuted their touted policy of pacifying the islands with kindness; it refuted their public claims that the policy was succeeding. Root publicly disapproved of Miles's letter, but the cat was out of the bag, with the result that in late March Congress began to make inquiries. Because the deep animosity between Roosevelt and Miles had not yet become public knowledge, Roosevelt said nothing. But, as was his wont, he wrote letters to many people, castigating Miles in vituperative and often–inaccurate terms.

Miles had one weapon. He could not openly defy the president, but he could—and did—testify in Congress against the administration's bill to reorganize the Army. A general staff, Miles insisted, might be appropriate for military powers such as France and Germany, but for a small army such as that of the United States, it would be inconsistent with the country's democratic principles. Miles was willing to stay small.

Finally, a reasonable solution presented itself. Root sent Miles to Manila as an "inspector," not to replace Taft and Chaffee. That mission occupied some months. On Miles's return home, Root successfully encouraged him to take a junket in the form of a trip around the world. Miles, in his glory, was feted in China, Japan, and Russia. He crossed the vast distance from Vladivostok to Europe mostly on the Russian Trans–Siberian Railway. By the time he returned to Washington from Europe, Miles had only a few months left to serve as general in chief. Those months were uneventful. Root's law was passed.

One of Roosevelt's most spectacular personal achievements during his presidency lay in his role in bringing about an end to the Russo–Japanese War in 1905. The peace that Roosevelt brokered had mixed results in the end, but at the time his accomplishment was viewed by all with universal acclaim.

The war between Russia and Japan was small by European standards, as nearly all the action was concentrated largely around a single city, Port Arthur, China. It was significant principally because it established Japan as a power on the world stage.

By way of background, Japan had long been viewed in Western circles as a relatively insignificant country. By the turn of the century, however, it was developing a degree of hegemony in the Far East and had participated in the eight–nation rescue expedition that freed the Forbidden City in the 1900 Boxer Rebellion. Still, Czar Nicholas of Russia did not consider Japan capable of interfering with his ambitions to move into this part of the world. Other nations found no reason to disagree with him.

By 1904 two issues pertaining to the czar's ambitions were giving the Japanese cause for concern. One was the Russian progress in building a Trans–Siberian Railway from Moscow to Vladivostok and the Sea of Japan. The other was a Russian troop buildup in Manchuria that came to some 180,000 men, a force far stronger than necessary to maintain law and order in that desolate country. Russia had previously made inroads in the region, and its ambition to attain the use of the warm–water Port Arthur was well known. In 1897 a Russian fleet had arrived at Port Arthur and forced the weak Chinese government to grant them a twenty–five–year lease. On its signing, Russia had sent troops to fortify the city and to build a railway from there to Mukden, Manchuria. Japan was also concerned that the Russians could move south from Manchuria to take Korea, a move that would be an obvious threat to nearby Japan. Negotiations over territorial issues had begun during 1902, with the Russians making the mistake of supposing they were dealing with a weak and timid power.

On February 8, 1904, the Japanese decided that the time had come for action. The Imperial Navy attacked the Russian Far East Fleet at Port Arthur without warning, badly damaging two battleships. The result was a formal declaration of war and a naval battle at Port Arthur. The results were indecisive, but the Russians were thenceforth unable to use Port Arthur for commercial purposes. Even their battle fleet took refuge in the port.

The war that ensued saw a series of victories for the Japanese. In April and May 1904, they repelled a Russian ground invasion of Korea and even crossed the Yalu River to create a bridgehead in Manchuria. But the focus of the fighting remained Port Arthur, where the Japanese, advancing by land, towed artillery pieces to the heights surrounding the city and destroyed the entire Russian fleet.

That series of Japanese victories should have ended the war, but the Russians refused to give up. The czar sent army reinforcements across the Trans–Siberian Railway and dispatched their Baltic Fleet of eight battleships. In late–May 1905, the Imperial Russian Navy was defeated at Tsushima by a smaller Japanese fleet on the high seas. As a result, an angry and frustrated Russian public staged riots in Moscow that have generally been regarded as the beginning of the downfall of the Romanov House in 1917.

The fighting in the Russo–Japanese War was essentially over, but the negotiators for the two sides could not settle on the terms for peace. At this point, Roosevelt stepped in and offered to mediate in the capacity of a private citizen; the president of the United States possessed no formal authority over either power. Posing as a private citizen was only a facade; it was only his position as president of the United States that caused either side to consider his offer.

The Russian and Japanese governments accepted Roosevelt's offer, and their emissaries arrived at Sagamore Hill in September 1905. Roosevelt had arranged accommodations for the delegates at the nearby naval base at Portsmouth, New Hampshire. There the two sides negotiated, with Roosevelt himself dropping in from time to time to assist. The treaty was signed on September 5, 1905.

Considering the overwhelming victories attained by the Japanese army and navy, the peace terms reached at Portsmouth were surprisingly generous to the Russians. The provisions required them to cede their twenty–five–year lease on Port Arthur to the Japanese. They were also required to give up the southern half of the island of Sakhalin and to recognize Japanese dominance of Korea. But two concessions originally demanded by the Japanese were refused. One was an indemnity for the war, which the czar refused to pay. The other was the Japanese demand for the northern half of Sakhalin. In both cases, Roosevelt supported the Russians, thus planting in Japan the seeds of hostility toward the United States that finally broke out at Pearl Harbor in 1941.

Roosevelt had achieved a creditable accomplishment, for which he was justifiably awarded the Nobel Peace Prize in 1907. He did not, however, accept the prize until after the end of his presidential administration, in 1910. And even then he turned over the cash award of thirty–five thousand dollars to charity.

Roosevelt did much in domestic matters during his nearly two terms in office as president. Such matters as conservation of natural resources, trust busting, and beginning the Panama Canal come to mind. His last memorable act, however, was again in his role as commander in chief, the dispatch of the "Great White Fleet" around the world in the waning days of his administration.

Always anxious to demonstrate to the world that the United States was to be counted as a major power, Roosevelt had long thought of making a naval demonstration during his term in office. In late 1907, with only a little more than a year left, he put that idea into effect. He decided to send a fleet of sixteen battleships around the world. Although many in Congress protested on the basis of cost, Roosevelt was determined.

On December 16, 1907, the first contingent of battleships departed Norfolk and headed south around Cape Horn, with its first–leg destination San

Francisco,[9] all ships bearing the peacetime white. It was an impressive formation; nearly all the battleships had been constructed since the Spanish–American War. At San Francisco, the fleet was consolidated, and it departed across the Pacific on July 7, 1908. It visited Auckland, Sydney, Manila, Yokohama, and Ceylon, arriving in Egypt on January 3, 1909. Two significant events occurred during this part of the odyssey: the people of Japan, still unhappy with Roosevelt as the result of the Treaty of Portsmouth, greeted the fleet with new respect, even enthusiasm. Second, while in the Mediterranean, Admiral Charles S. Sperry was able to detach a couple of ships to aid in rescue efforts from a serious eruption of Mount Etna, Sicily.

The first elements of the Great White Fleet completed the voyage when they arrived at Hampton Roads on February 22, 1909, calculated to fall on George Washington's birthday. Roosevelt, with less than three weeks left in the office of president, was there on hand. Typically, he made the most of it.

Fourteen thousand sailors had participated in this voyage, considered by many to be an impossible venture. A jubilant Theodore Roosevelt ended his career as commander in chief with his usual flamboyance and éclat. The public in general wished him well.

But not everybody. Two days after Roosevelt left office, the anti–imperialist Mark Twain wrote a scathing letter to a friend:

> For seven years this country has lain smothering under the incubus in the person of President Roosevelt. Thanks be we got rid of this disastrous burden day before yesterday, at last. Forever? Probably not. Probably for only a brief breathing spell, wherein, under Mr. Taft, we may hope to get back some of our health—four years. We may expect to have Mr. Roosevelt sitting on us again, the presidential burden that a hostile Providence could impose upon us for our sins.
>
> Our people have adored this showy charlatan as perhaps no imposter of his brood has been adored since the Golden Calf, so it is to be expected that the Nation will want him back again after he has done hunting other wild animals heroically in Africa, with the safeguard and advertising equipment of a park of artillery and a brass band.[10]

In referring to the popular Theodore Roosevelt as an "incubus," Mark Twain was representing only a small minority. But in his predictions as to Roosevelt's actions in the future, he was prescient.

9. Because the Panama Canal was still under construction, the fleet was forced to cross through the treacherous Strait of Magellan.

10. Twain to B. F. N., March 6, 1909, sent as an enclosure to a letter sent by the recipient to the *New York Times*, May 28, 1912.

(Top) Theodore Roosevelt in the Dakotas, courtesy of Library of Congress.

(Bottom) Leonard Wood, courtesy of Library of Congress

(Top) Theodore Roosevelt, Rough Rider, courtesy of Library of Congress.

(Bottom) Major General William R. Shafter, courtesy of Library of Congress.

(Top) Rear Admiral William T. Sampson, courtesy of Library of Congress.

(Bottom) Calixto Garcia, courtesy of Library of Congress.

(Top) Portrait of Major General Leonard Wood, USV, courtesy of Library of Congress.

(Bottom) President William McKinley, courtesy of Library of Congress.

(Top) President Theodore Roosevelt, courtesy of Library of Congress.

(Bottom) Secretary of War Elihu Root, courtesy of Library of Congress.

(Top) Major General Nelson A. Miles, courtesy of Library of Congress.

(Bottom) General John J. Pershing, courtesy of Library of Congress.

(Top) President Woodrow Wilson, courtesy of Library of Congress.

(Bottom) Secretary of War Newton D. Baker, courtesy of Library of Congress.

12

THE RISE OF JOHN J. PERSHING

While Theodore Roosevelt was in his first term as president and Leonard Wood was governing Cuba, another figure was rising on the scene: John J. Pershing, captain, 10th Cavalry.

Nobody at that time could possibly predict Pershing's distinguished future. Fewer yet could imagine that twelve years later, Leonard Wood and even Theodore Roosevelt would be his supplicants. Although they were all about the same age, Pershing's rank was lowly—a captain, in contrast to a president and a major general. Granted, within the Army itself, Pershing was no nonentity, but to the public he was an unknown.

Pershing never showed any friendly feelings for either Roosevelt or Wood, even though the three men had been within yards of each other in the charge up Kettle and San Juan Hills in Cuba. Certainly, he held neither in any awe. He may, in fact, have been one of those regulars who advised against awarding Roosevelt the Congressional Medal of Honor. Pershing was always conscious that the 10th Cavalry, in which he himself was a lieutenant, had charged ahead of the Rough Riders in the attack and had taken casualties far heavier than those of the Rough Riders. But regardless of Pershing's personal feelings toward Roosevelt and Wood, he was quite willing to accept what favors either had to offer.

Pershing's first significant assignment after the Cuban campaign came in late 1899 when he was ordered, at his own request, to the Philippines. He went as a major of volunteers but was soon reverted to captain, Regular Army. He was then assigned to the headquarters in Manila.

Whether by orders or his own initiative, Pershing set out to study the complicated situation in the Moro Province of the Southern Islands. By then resistance from the *insurrectos* was wavering, but another set of antagonists was still there. Those enemies, the Moros, were fanatic Mohammedans who did not consider themselves Filipinos. They were no newcomers. Their identification began as early as the thirteenth century with the arrival of Muslim missionaries. Thus, they had been established in the Philippines long before Magellan had arrived at Cebu in 1521. They had never accepted the authority of the Catholic Spanish in Manila, and when the Americans had come in 1898, they had expected to be recognized as independent. Such hopes had been shattered, however, when the Treaty of Paris had ceded them to the Americans along with the rest of the Philippines. So the American problem was to induce the Moros to assist them in subduing the waning *insurrectos* and then to settle peacefully under a somewhat loose titular rule of the United States.

It was a difficult problem, because the Moros were (and are) a fierce, unruly people. To further complicate matters, the Moro community itself was far from monolithic. In general terms, they fell into two major groups, the Moros of Sulu and those of Mindanao. The Sulu group inhabited an island chain of that name, which ran down from Mindanao toward Borneo, with the capital at Jolo. The other Moro group, which inhabited the large island of Mindanao, was divided administratively by the Americans into three major provinces, Zamboanga, Davao, and Cotabato. But those names were nearly meaningless, because Moros there were fragmented into small independent tribes, each headed by a *datu,* a term that translates roughly into the word *chief.* No cohesion existed among the hundreds of *datus.* Had the *datus* been able to unify their total of twenty thousand warriors, the Americans could never have subdued them with the three regiments stationed on Mindanao. But there was no fear of that happening.[1]

Pershing studied these fierce, wild, and dirty people and even learned their language. From what he could learn, he concluded that the Moros could be dealt with in much the same way as the Indians of the American West. They would respond to kindness, but would fight to the death against any intruders they did not trust.

1. "[The Moro] seemed incomprehensible and lost to decency and humanity, the Moro, a believer in polygamy and slavery with filed teeth chewing betel nuts so that his saliva was blood red, a ferocious pirate terrifying Christian Filipinos with his terrible weapons so skillfully wielded. He had no government beyond shifting allegiances to tribal chieftains bearing feudal–like the most august of titles, maharaja, sultan, but who lived in bamboo shacks set a few feet above the ground littered with waste, and whose adherents could amount to no more that a few hundred souls. In that world murder was lightly regarded. Girls were sold at birth for later delivery. In Moroland it was held as faith that Americans had cloven feet." Gene Smith, *Until the Last Trumpet Sounds,* 58.

Pershing's studies affected his future. In November 1901, the new commander of the Philippine Department, Brigadier General George W. Davis, decided that his new qualifications might be of practical use in helping pacify those Moros who lived around Lake Lanao, a body of water about twenty miles by twelve miles. It was the main hotbed in north–central Mindanao, and Davis assigned Pershing to command a small post at Iligan, on the north shore. There relations were particularly hostile.

On arrival at Iligan, Pershing found the garrison in deplorable condition. Morale was low and discipline was lax. A martinet, he quickly dealt with those conditions, at the same time setting about his real job of developing peaceful relations with the local Moro *datus*.

Pershing gave his all to the mission of establishing trust, using methods theretofore unheard of. He started out by inviting local *datus* individually to his headquarters, giving them presents, and treating them as equals. He took the risk of returning the visits of any *datus* who had come to see him. In doing so, he dispensed with the usual security guard, traveling alone and unarmed. So successful was he that after he had been there a year, the local *datus*, in a solemn ceremony, named him as an honorary *datu* himself, an honor never accorded to any other American.

In April 1902, General Adna R. Chaffee, now commanding the Philippine Department, gave Pershing a very special assignment, the command of a much larger post, Camp Vicars, on the southern shore of the lake. So important was this command that Pershing was told to report to General Chaffee himself, bypassing the governor of the province. It was a prestigious assignment for an officer who, though a veteran of seventeen years' service, was still a captain. It included infantry, cavalry, artillery, and engineers, five to six hundred men. Pershing's predecessor had been a full colonel, now a brigadier.

Pershing remained at Camp Vicars for an entire year, and of that year he spent eleven months courting the local *datus* and gaining their confidence, as he had done at Iligan. On July 4, 1902, for example, he gave a celebration that included seven hundred Moro guests. But not all the *datus* showed up. Some remained hostile. In September, therefore, Pershing conducted a couple of expeditions against those who remained recalcitrant. His operations were canceled, however, by an outbreak of cholera among the civilian population and by a series of torrential rains.

By early 1903, Pershing seems to have come to a gloomy conclusion that too much Moro resistance remained. Risking his life among the Moro *datus* to make friends was not reducing the numbers of those still following their old ways. From a personal point of view, his efforts were not being appreciated. Battles, he concluded, had to be reported in the papers to call attention to the progress he was making. Accordingly, he decided that in April, he would make a march around Lake Lanao as a show of force. The ostensible purpose of the pilgrimage was to resume friendships with the friendly *datus.* But many *datus* were still hostile, so he knew that he would meet resistance from at least some of those chiefs.

Pershing's preparations were elaborate. To differentiate between friend and potential foe, he announced his route ahead of time and emphasized the peaceful nature of the march. He asked the local *datus* to display American flags or white flags if they were friendly and red flags if they were not. Once his march began, he found that the vast majority of cases displayed white flags. It was only at a place called Bacolod that he had a real fight. It lasted two days, and by its end 150 or more Moros lay dead. Pershing had only a couple of men wounded.

To what degree Pershing was seeking attention cannot be judged, but he did in fact receive it. Operations around Lake Lanao finally received due notice in the United States. Pershing obviously played a part. On June 22, 1903, the *New York Times* carried a prominent story with the headline "Pershing's Story of Lanao Fight; Commander of Bacolod Expedition Sends Account of It to Friend."

The source of the story was a personal letter that Pershing had written to a friend. It was a hefty two–column account in which he described the scene at Bacolod, a strong defensive position called a *cotta,* which consisted of an earthen fortress around a village, surrounded by a moat thirty–five feet wide and forty feet deep. Pershing described the methods he used in attacking it. After securing the high ground around the *cotta,* he brought up artillery pieces and bombarded the position for two whole days. He stressed in his letter that he had left an escape lane for the evacuation of women and children. His unbelievably one–sided losses were later essentially confirmed by the Moros. In the letter, he somewhat disingenuously asserted that all the credit belonged to his superiors. He concluded grandly, "There will never again be any continued opposition nor any general opposition. It is needless for me to say to you that I am gratified at the outcome. From Bacolod north to Marahui there were more United States flags displayed than I expected existed in this country. I have been here nearly two years and can but feel that this is the largest success that has been made in the Islands."[2]

Given the American contempt for the Moros, Pershing's harsh measures were considered quite humane. He may have been overly optimistic in his

2. *New York Times,* June 22, 1903.

assessment of the long-term effects of his exploits, but he had performed a tour de force. He was now a national hero.

When Pershing's normal Philippine tour ended in 1903, he took his time returning home, traveling by way of Europe. He arrived in Washington in July, where he learned to his surprise that he was now noted, if not famous. Rumors were rife that he was being considered for promotion to the grade of brigadier general. Secretary of War Elihu Root, in fact, had let slip a remark at a party that such an action was under consideration.

Pershing was no shrinking violet in promoting his case for such a promotion. Besides the letter he had written describing his exploits, which had received much publicity, he solicited recommendations from other officers who had witnessed his success. The matter now reached the desk of the president.

The pressure to make such an unusual promotion put President Roosevelt in a rather uncomfortable bind. Personally, as an advocate of exerting American force, he favored granting some sort of reward. The matter was not nearly so simple as it seemed, however.

The easy way to honor Pershing would be to present him with a medal. However, Roosevelt wisely realized that such a transitory reward would not be lasting.[3] Another device, a reasonable one, would be to promote him to major or lieutenant colonel, appropriate because Pershing's command at Lake Lanao had comprised about 550 men, or about half the size of a regiment. But regulations did not permit him to promote an officer to those grades. Army regulations, passed by Congress and carrying the force of law, denied the president authority to promote within a branch—that is, up to the grade of colonel. He could appoint Pershing to brigadier general, but not to major, lieutenant colonel, or colonel.

Roosevelt consulted the secretary of war. Root was favorably disposed toward Pershing, but he considered a jump in grade to brigadier general to be unwise. Not only would it cause too much unhappiness in the officer ranks; Root had another, older, officer whom he considered more deserving.[4] Roosevelt was temporarily defeated, and he allowed the matter to drop. Pershing would go unrewarded for the time being.

Pershing was too good a soldier to allow rejection for promotion to affect the performance of his duties. However, a new twist came into his life when, as a forty-five-year-old bachelor, he became enamored of the

3. The Medal of Honor, which he still coveted, was an exception.

4. Colonel William J. Barrie Jr.

young daughter of Senator Francis Warren of Wyoming, the chairman of the Armed Forces Committee. Suspicious though the matter may have appeared, the mutual attraction seems to have been a true case of love at first sight. Moreover, the aggressor in promoting the relationship was the young lady herself, Helen Frances (Frankie) Warren, a warm, vivacious girl, who had recently, at age twenty–three, graduated from Wellesley. Pershing certainly returned her affection, but at first he held back, concerned about his financial situation as a mere captain. Miss Warren would have none of that inhibition; she made it clear that she already possessed an inheritance enough to make them comfortable.

The two agreed to marry, and a lavish wedding was held on January 26, 1905. It was reported that forty–five hundred invitations were sent out, and in honor of the occasion the United States Senate delayed opening that day in order to allow its members to attend.[5] President Roosevelt and his wife were present. It was rare indeed for such attention to be accorded a captain, but Senator Warren was not one to hide his affections for his daughter, and he was influential.

He was so influential, in fact, that he seems to have had an effect on Pershing's career prospects. He dropped a broad hint to Roosevelt that some of the legislation the administration wanted might be passed more easily if his new son–in–law would be made a general. Roosevelt gave in, and Pershing was promoted from captain to brigadier general, bypassing 862 officers senior to him, 257 of whom were captains. The nomination was made on September 20, 1905, and though it was confirmed by the Senate, it predictably caused an uproar in the Army officer corps. Fortunately, by the time the promotion had been confirmed, Pershing and his new bride had left Washington for Tokyo, where Pershing was to be military attaché and an observer in the 1904–5 Russo–Japanese War.

Pershing was away from center scene, and he did not come back seriously into Roosevelt's life for more than a decade.

5. Smith, *Until the Last Trumpet Sounds*, 82.

13

Wood in the Philippines, 1902–8

In late–May 1902, Major General Leonard Wood and his wife set sail from Havana, bound for the United States. With Cuba now an independent nation, his duties as the American governor had come to an end. The Cubans gave the Woods a lavish send–off, a tribute to the man who had governed them for three years.

Wood was satisfied with the job he had done as governor, but he carried regret. The United States, he believed, had terminated the occupation too soon. Like many Americans—and nearly all Army officers—he held a low opinion of the ability of brown people to govern themselves. While aboard ship, he wrote in his diary, "Once in my stateroom with the doors closed I felt for the first time a feeling of complete relief and satisfaction that the work was done and the transfer over, although I felt and feel it would have been much better for the Cuban people if we had remained several years longer and give [*sic*] them a chance to settle down on a much more sound basis."[1]

Wood was in no hurry for reassignment. He spent some time around Washington and then joined two other officers on a trip to Europe to witness the annual military maneuvers. They first visited France and Spain, and on August 17, 1902, they arrived in Germany, where some forty thousand in the kaiser's elite army divisions were conducting maneuvers. He was not treated as an ordinary major general of volunteers. He enjoyed an elevated status among the

1. Wood diary, May 20, 1902, Wood Papers, cited in Jack McCallum, *Leonard Wood: Rough Rider, Surgeon, Architect of American Imperialism,* 197.

Europeans because they viewed Wood's previous position as governor of Cuba with great respect. To them, he had ruled a territory larger than many European countries; he was a proconsul. To the Americans, on the other hand, he had been merely a general performing a special kind of duty.

In the course of witnessing the German maneuvers, Wood was afforded the opportunity to converse at some length with Kaiser Wilhelm II. Though very different men, they were both by nature imperialists, and they seemed to enjoy each other. Wood later wrote admiringly that the kaiser's mastery of the English language was better than that of King George V of England, whom he later visited.

On return to Washington, Wood consulted with Roosevelt, not the War Department, about his next assignment. Together they decided that he should take command of the Moro Province in the Southern Islands of the Philippines. On the face of it, this post as a mere provincial governor seemed to be a demotion from his previous position as governor–general of an entire country. And so it was, technically. But the Moro Province was the only area of the Philippines where fighting was still going on, and Wood carried a yen to get back to straight soldiering. Besides, the present governor of the Philippines, William Howard Taft, was expected to leave Manila soon. When that event occurred, Wood might step up and take Taft's place as governor or commander of the Philippine Division—or so Wood understood Roosevelt's promises.

As he well knew, Wood had enemies that could exert themselves because Roosevelt had just nominated him for promotion to major general in the United States Army,[2] a substantial step up from his current status as a volunteer. This action required the consent of Congress. With any other officer, such a confirmation would be routine, especially because it conformed to custom. As a result of his earlier meteoric rise, Wood was the senior brigadier general in the Army, and because a vacancy had opened up, the recommendation fell into a normal order of seniority.

Wood's case, however, was unusual. Many Democrats would oppose him as a personal friend of Roosevelt's, and some Republicans, such as Mark Hanna, joined in opposition, as Hanna was a political enemy of Roosevelt and Henry Cabot Lodge. There were also senior Army officers who still resented Wood's appointment as governor of Cuba back in 1899. One of these was Major General John R. Brooke, who considered himself the victim of a conspiracy. There was also General James H. Wilson, who had considered himself the logical contender for that position. And finally, there was former postmaster Estes

2. Wood's two stars had previously been in the volunteers.

Rathbone, whom Wood had jailed for corruption and who sought revenge. Rathbone was, incidentally, strongly supported by Hanna.

Wood was undaunted by the prospect of confronting this array of antagonists; he never shrank from a fight. But Roosevelt saw such a confrontation as a potential political disaster. True friend that he was, Roosevelt was not blind to the prospect that Wood's touch of arrogance would stir up unnecessary trouble. Accordingly, Roosevelt ordered Wood to depart Washington for the Philippines before the hearings began. Roosevelt would fight the battle himself.

Roosevelt had every reason for concern; his own interests were at stake. In nominating Wood for promotion, he was expending a good deal of the political capital he needed to secure the Republican presidential nomination in 1904. Had he been a president elected in his own right in 1900, he would have faced negligible opposition. But he had not, and he knew that no previous president who had succeeded from the vice presidency to the presidency had been seriously considered for a term of his own.[3] Roosevelt was an exceedingly popular man compared to the others, but his nomination was not ensured; political capital was still important to him.

So Wood left Washington for the Philippines with his confirmation by the Senate still pending. Mrs. Wood and the family stayed behind.

On his arrival in Manila in the late summer of 1902, Wood was greeted warmly by Governor William H. Taft. As there was no reason for hurry to assume his provincial post at Zamboanga, he stayed around the capital for a couple of weeks, studying the Moros and the entire region of the Southern Islands. What he learned through studying the Moros convinced him that his position as governor of the Moro Province would be an entirely different experience from what he had just left. In Cuba his main job had been one of reconstruction. At Zamboanga there would be some of that, but his main challenge would be one of subduing one hundred thousand fierce and rebellious people, about twenty thousand of whom were warriors.

By way of review, the Moro Province was theoretically broken down into three parts: the Sulu Archipelago, the Lake Lanao Group in Western Mindanao, and the Cotobato Group in the eastern part of Mindanao.[4] To subdue these areas, Wood had three regiments. Because he needed to be able to

3. John Tyler, James Fillmore, Andrew Johnson, and Chester Arthur.

4. McCallum lists five groups, the Maguindanaos at Cotabato, the Yakans of Basilan Island, the Maranaos on Lake Lanao, the Samals on the Zamboanga Peninsula, and the Sulus of the Sulu Archipelago and Palawan. Ibid., 205.

concentrate military force in trouble spots on short notice, he concentrated them around Zamboanga. The *datu* organization that Pershing was working with was actually greatly intact, despite Black Jack's efforts. And the sultan of Sulu in the town of Jolo was a figurehead, ignored by if not laughed at by the Sulu Moros.

Wood had many precedents to study, the most significant being that of Brigadier General Jacob Smith, at Samar in 1901, where he killed an estimated two thousand Moros. Smith's reported order to shoot all males over the age of ten may have been misread, but it was accepted as true. It was Smith's harsh approach rather than Taft's (and Pershing's) that Wood chose to follow.

On August 6, 1902, Wood assumed formal command of the Moro Province, with headquarters at Zamboanga. The circumstances of living were exceedingly agreeable. The town is located at the southern tip of a peninsula often compared to the claw of a crab, three-thousand-foot mountains to the east and beautiful blue waters to the west. The headquarters building itself was located only a few miles from the wharf, near Fort Pilar. Both the fort and the luxurious general's quarters were ancient, having been built by the Spaniards at about the same time that the pilgrims landed at Plymouth Rock from England. It was a post that a less motivated general might have simply luxuriated in, the main hardship being the absence of his family. The Moros, who constituted only 5 percent of the population (but owned about half the land), were doing most of their fighting among themselves—the rest of the Filipinos were well subdued, and they respected the might of the Americans even though they naturally resented being ruled, no matter how loosely, by any foreigners—American, Spanish, or even Filipinos from Manila.

But ease and comfort were the last things on Wood's mind. Within two days of arriving at Zamboanga, he boarded a small dispatch boat to make an inspection of the cities under his control. At one point, he turned into the mouth of the Agus River, which led eastward toward the northern shore of Lake Lanao. The trip took him through forests and later into an open plain. On both sides of the river were deceptively peaceful-looking villages, where lived the *datus* that were always at war with one another. Wood's own observations were revealing:

> Cultivation here is very well done and the Moro looks fairly thrifty. If the intense family fighting can be stopped, great progress can be made by these people, but they are consistently fighting with each other. Each man's cotta is a fortified establishment, fronted by a tremendous ditch and a high parapet which is planted thickly with prickly bamboo. The work is generally entered by a narrow bamboo bridge of one or two poles crossing the moat and leading

> to a narrow tunnel–like entrance to the parapet, which is big enough for one person, so these places are rather difficult to take.

He added in a letter to his wife, still in the United States, that this was wild country and that it would be years before they could govern themselves.[5] In that respect, at least, the Filipinos resembled the Cubans in Wood's mind.

The command of the Moro Province involved more than soldiering; it involved diplomacy as well. Early in his tenure, Wood made a trip to Borneo to visit the British governor on matters of mutual interest—specifically how to cope with those seagoing Moros who recognized no boundaries. Pillage was probably at the top of the list of topics for discussion, and next was the Moro habit of holding slaves, an activity that went against the principles of both Britain and the United States. His conference in Borneo complete, Wood then made a tour of the Celebes Sea before returning to Zamboanga.

From what he had seen on his various inspections of the Moro region, the new major general (as of August 8) concluded that the only way to pacify the Moros was by fear, not kindness. To that end, he set out to instill in them a respect for American might, by paying a series of formal calls on various powerful *datus.* Unlike Pershing, however, he took with him enough force to provide for his own safety and more, the purpose being to make the Moros witness for themselves the weapons they would face if involved in battle with their masters. Convinced that he had not taken enough men with him on his first forays, he took a party of about 450 men to Jolo.[6]

As a matter of protocol, Wood first visited the sultan, for whom he had a special message. An earlier American commander had unwisely signed a treaty with the sultan, granting the Moros authority to continue their old ways of depredation and slavery, and Wood had to straighten that misconception out, which he did.

The sultan of Sulu claimed a bloodline running back through Muhammad and Ishmael, and even to Adam, but as previously noted the man who filled the position in 1903 was no tower of strength.[7] Wood therefore held only a short conference with the sultan and then called together a group of powerful *datus* and laid down the law: He announced that the Moros were now under the authority of a "new and strong country that would insist on tranquil-

5. Hagedorn, *Leonard Wood, a Biography,* 2:6.

6. Four companies of infantry, a detachment of cavalry, and a battery of the fearsome Gatling guns. Ibid., 8.

7. His mother was a different matter. It was said that she had procured a considerable quantity of poison as a means of ensuring her weak son's retention of his throne.

ity and enforce the laws prohibiting slavery." Resistance to the United States would be the equivalent of suicide. Raids on Borneo would have to stop, and the Moro habit of *juramentado*[8] would have to cease.[9] Because the perpetrators of these suicide acts would be killed, Wood emphasized that the *datus* and their priests would be held responsible for such acts as severely as if they had performed the acts in person.

As a final gesture, Wood decided to visit the sultan's brother, a stronger man who kept his base a few miles from Jolo and who reportedly held the real power. So Wood assembled a force of three infantry companies, two Gatling guns, and forty mules to find him. The man evaded meeting by offering all sorts of excuses, but Wood's representatives cornered him and the men conferred. Wood had done all he could. He had made his points clear and had demonstrated a show of force. He once more headed back to Zamboanga.

In keeping with his conviction that the Moros were hopelessly intransigent, Wood adopted a policy of annihilation whenever he attacked a given *cotta*. He did not intend to lose many American lives, and his tactics were therefore designed to take full advantage of his superiority in artillery. He would, in attacking a *cotta,* saturate its parapets with guns from a range of about fifteen hundred yards, pulverizing the crests to the extent that he was sure that all Moro warriors would be killed. Then, with his infantry force, usually three or four companies, he would make his way up to the rim surrounding the village. He would then fire with small arms and Gatling guns into the village until he was sure that practically all of the occupants were dead, including women and children. His troops would then go through the village and make sure that there were no survivors.

Wood could hardly be blamed for the deaths of women, because many of them would don black clothing and, showing no sign of their gender, fight with the men to the death. Thus, it was only the children who were unjustly killed. As a rule, Wood's losses in Americans would be only a handful. His tactics were shocking to many Americans, but they were effective.

In early–April 1904, Wood conducted one of his campaigns around Lake Lanao, the scene where Pershing had operated with minimum loss of life a couple of years earlier. Having finished, he returned to Zamboanga and thence to Manila to meet his family, whom he had not seen for many months. On arrival he learned that President Roosevelt, for some reason, had decided to

8. Suicide raids against Christians.

9. McCallum, *Leonard Wood,* 214.

appoint Major General Henry C. Corbin, rather than himself, as commander of the Philippine Division. Wood wrote a testy letter to the president in protest.[10] Roosevelt in turn reminded Wood that he, Roosevelt, had just risked his own political future by supporting Wood's promotion. Wood apparently saw the light and retreated. He took his family to Zamboanga, where they could enjoy a peaceful domestic life for a while. It turned out that Corbin's health degenerated, and Wood assumed command of the Philippine Division.

Wood did not confine his interests to Philippine affairs. In 1905 a disagreement arose between the United States and China over American immigration policy on the West Coast of the United States. The Burlingame Treaty of 1904 allowed the United States to restrict or prohibit the entrance of Chinese laborers to the country's shores. The Chinese government did not take American racial insults lying down. Its government slapped a boycott on American goods. Although the matter was hardly in Wood's sphere, he and Roosevelt corresponded extensively on the subject. Of the two, Wood was far the more adamant. He advocated exclusion of Chinese immigration and went so far as to advocate taking action against the Chinese homeland. On January 7, 1906, he wrote Roosevelt, stating that he had prepared a regiment and it was ready to sail. A month later, he declared that he had five thousand troops ready to go and further volunteered that the Navy was prepared to cooperate. Fortunately, Roosevelt kept a cool head, and in a couple of months the pressure from Chinese merchants caused the blockade to subside. Roosevelt had set the policy, and Wood had kept the president abreast of his current capabilities.[11]

The climax of Wood's service in the Philippines came in 1906. As a result of his destruction among the *cottas* of both Mindanao and Sulu, many Moros had been left homeless. At Jolo, therefore, a group of such people had taken refuge inside an extinct crater named Mount Dajo, a two–thousand–foot mountain about six miles to the southwest of the city. These fugitives came from all directions, and by any civilized standards they were a sorry lot. As Hermann Hagedorn, Wood's most admiring biographer, describes them, they were people who "have sought refuge in the crater of Bud Dajo. . . . They are the rag–tag and bob–tail remnants of two or three revolts, the black sheep of a dozen folds, rebels against the poll–tax, die–hards against the American occupation, recognizing no datus and condemned by the stable elements among the Moros themselves. They have been permitted to remain in their fastness

10. Ibid., 221.
11. Lane, *Armed Progressive,* 136–37.

[fortified place] only because Wood and [Colonel Hugh] Scott have hoped that time might work soothingly upon their militancy."[12]

These refugees were lawless, but how dangerous they were might be open to question. One thing was certain, however: they intended to stay where they were, even if it resulted in another Alamo or Masada. Their determination frightened what Moros had been subdued, and several delegations of friendly *datus* reportedly urged them to disperse and return to their original homes. But they did not. Although they made promises, they stayed in place after each harvest and continued to fortify the position.

There was no unanimity of opinion among Americans and Moros about the danger that the refugees of Bud Dajo posed to the nearby more "peaceful" Moros. Colonel Hugh Scott believed that they could be induced to leave. And although they postured and claimed their intention to commit depredations around the Jolo region, little damage had ever been positively identified, though they did venture out of their stronghold in small groups.

The Bud Dajo *cotta* was built on an unusually strong piece of terrain. From about five hundred feet from the crest of the surrounding rim, the slope ran about sixty degrees, and near the top it became nearly vertical. Attacking troops had to climb the branches of the trees that grew horizontally out of the ground. To assault the crater required troops in the best of condition.

By February 1906, Wood had finally lost his patience, and he decided to attack the position. Despite the arguments of Scott, who tried to dissuade him, Wood gave a direct order on March 5 for an American force of about one hundred men to attack the Mount Dajo *cotta,* using three trails at night. Wood supervised the action from a small boat at the base of the crater. The Moro defenders—women indiscernible from the men and just as vicious—poured fire on them. To Wood's frustration, the American troops failed to make it up the crest on the first day. On the second day, however, a group of constabulary reached the top. They managed to hoist a howitzer, which created a barrage that the defenders could not resist. As the survivors tumbled into the crater, American troops followed and then, in order to minimize friendly casualties, pounded the helpless people in the village below until they were sure that only a few of them were still alive. American casualties came to eighteen killed and fifty–two wounded.[13]

Wood realized that the brutal measures would be criticized at home, and he attempted to play down the affair. Inevitably, however, word leaked, and

12. Hagedorn, *Leonard Wood, a Biography,* 2:64.
13. Lane, *Armed Progressive,* 128.

the action was reported in the United States. Before that word came, President Roosevelt, impressed by Wood's description of the hardships and dangers his troops had faced, sent a message of congratulations. The *New York Times* saw the irony. On March 9, 1906, its headlines blazoned:

> WOMEN AND CHILDREN KILLED
> IN MORO BATTLE
> PRESIDENT WIRES CONGRATULATIONS
> TO TROOPS[14]

Secretary of War William Howard Taft, always an advocate of humane treatment of enemies, was not impressed. He sent a discomfiting message to Wood, demanding an explanation. Wood suppressed his anger enough to make his case, and the incident was dropped for the moment. Some newsmen, however, filed records of it for future use.

Previous to the Mount Dajo massacre, Wood had, in addition to his duties as commander of the Philippine Division, retained his status as governor of the Moro Province. In that capacity, he called together a group of friendly (or cowed) *datus* and persuaded them to endorse his conduct of the Dajo episode. In April, assuming that the Moros had been pacified, he turned over those duties to his chief assistant, the intellectual Tasker Bliss. He could now concentrate on his role with the division in Manila.

One of Wood's concerns as division commander was the quality of the officer corps under his command. He observed, probably with reason, that the War Department had a policy of sending him too many officers who were on their last tour before retirement or who were obviously short on ambition. It was not the top echelon that he was concerned about—both Hugh Scott and Tasker Bliss were future Army chiefs of staff—but those of field grade, major through colonel. He also argued for more troops on the basis that the Philippines were ideal as a training ground because of its large tracts of empty space. The War Department, however, did little.

Wood now ran into a new problem, this one involving the Navy, which was proposing to build a naval base at Olongapo, on Subic Bay, thirty-five miles northwest from Manila. Wood saw this as a threat. One of his concerns was strategic. He was convinced that in the event of war with Japan, the United States would be unable to control the South China Sea for at least the first phase. His own plans called for concentrating all of his fourteen thousand

14. Ibid., 128–29.

troops on Luzon in Fortress Manila, which included the bay and the small island of Corregidor, in the mouth of Manila Bay. He provided Corregidor with ammunition and provisions sufficient to hold out for eight months. He strongly recommended that the United States Asiatic Fleet, instead of splitting up between Manila Bay and the proposed base at Olongapo, should concentrate in Manila Bay and add its firepower to the guns of Corregidor in the defense of Manila. The Navy demurred, contending that the waters of the bay were too shallow.

Wood's other concern regarding Subic Bay was bureaucratic, fear that this proposed naval installation would draw resources from the Army. Not only was the budget for Philippine defense at stake, but the proposed naval base would require defense from an enemy approach by land. It would take ten thousand Army troops, he calculated. In addition, he visualized that the Navy might push to have the base defended by Marines, not by soldiers, thus drawing further on resources allocated to the Army.

As usual, Wood expressed his concerns in letters directly to Roosevelt. Roosevelt accepted this practice but disregarded Wood's protests over Olongapo. The Army–Navy Defense Board had agreed that the base should be built, and Roosevelt approved their findings. The president made one concession, however. The Army, not the Marine Corps, should defend it. When surveys of the high ground surrounding Subic Bay began, Wood concluded that ten thousand troops would not suffice. But his role in the controversy was over. Wood was a prophet without power.

During these last days of Wood's tenure in the Philippines, Roosevelt became more and more concerned about his friend's health, particularly the brain tumor that had been operated on previously. Wood scoffed at that concern, but he had no objections to returning to the United States, especially to the prestigious Eastern Department, with headquarters at Governors Island, in New York Harbor.

In making the appointment, however, Roosevelt exercised caution. He decided that the still controversial general should avoid reaching the United States before the presidential election of 1908. So Wood and his family delayed leaving Manila until February 1908. In doing so, they somewhat repeated their previous tour of Europe, witnessing maneuvers in both Germany and France and meeting with the kaiser once again. They arrived back in New York in early–November 1908. William Howard Taft, Roosevelt's protégé, had just been elected president of the United States by a large margin.

14

Chief of Staff

On November 9, 1908, Leonard Wood assumed command of the Eastern Department, US Army, a position next to that of the chief of staff in importance. As such, his authority spread from New England down to Florida and even to the Panama Canal. Such of the country's militia forces as were located in the East also came under his authority. From his office window on Governors Island, he could look across the water to the immense skyscrapers of New York. Yet he did not appear to be particularly enchanted by the prospect. As he wrote a friend, "I feel as though I have been relegated to the command of an old soldiers' home. . . . I have no doubt I will eventually find it a very interesting command when I get into the work but there is very little left to the Department Commander's initiative. . . . The numerous quasi–social obligations which one has to meet, such as public dinners, reviews of regiments in their armories, etc., will, I am sure, be tiresome to some degree."[1]

Despite Wood's gloomy mood, he soon made his presence felt, though speech making and writing were less exciting than field duty. Though a bit dull, however, life was not unpleasant. Wood and his wife were socially prominent in both New York and Washington, and on the side he managed to improve the athletic facilities at Governors Island itself. His proximity to New York made it easy for many old friends to drop in to visit. But, being the driving personality that he was, these activities were not enough.

1. Wood to Colonel James Harbord, November 14, 1908, cited in Hagedorn, *Leonard Wood, a Biography*, 2:84.

By this time, even more than Roosevelt, Wood was becoming an avid promoter of preparedness for war. From the days of Santiago in 1898, he had been realistic about America's military weakness compared to the countries of Europe, and that realization was now even more evident. He had made two trips to Europe and witnessed the maneuvers of both Germany and France, and the experiences had had an effect on him.

Wood was particularly dissatisfied with the quality of the Army officer corps. In August 1908, he had written Roosevelt, who was still president: "Forty per cent of our colonels and 30 per cent of our field officers would be a detriment to troops in a campaign simply because they are either worn out old men or because they were not promoted until their initiative was gone. We have the best material in the world for soldiers but it must be used at the right age and made to work."[2]

Wood was ahead of his time in identifying that problem. Only later, during the mobilization for the Great War, did the need to weed out incompetents become clear. He began a study of Army organization, especially the writings of Emory Upton, who had so influenced Elihu Root. He enthusiastically agreed on the need to develop the General Staff, but he disagreed with Upton's thesis that war was the business of generals and not of civilian superiors. An expanded Regular Army, he contended, would suffice to provide for the nation's need for its defense, but Wood visualized a far–greater need for trained troops. His view was that the Regular Army in peacetime should be small but highly trained for use as a cadre for a large reserve force. Wood's concept was to be borne out handsomely in the Great War.

Wood, however, was limited in what he himself could do about American weakness; broad policy was out of his purview as commander of the Eastern Department. However, he had enough resources available to enable him to stage a maneuver to test the country's military capacities. During the summer of 1909, he conducted a military exercise involving both regulars and National Guardsmen from New York and New England, with the Navy cooperating. The experience convinced him more than ever that US coastal defenses, which depended largely on monster artillery pieces guarding the harbors, were nearly useless. Several foreign nations, he believed, possessed the power to make amphibious landings at points other than these harbors and take the guns from the rear.

All in all, Wood was pleased with the maneuver, and he planned to follow up with others in future years. In this he was thwarted, however. Word came

2. Ibid., 86–87.

from his superiors in Washington to cease this activity. The field conditions were too strenuous on the National Guard troops.

In September 1909, Major General Franklin Bell, Army chief of staff, was due for retirement, making Wood the senior officer in the Army. Accordingly, President Taft, with the strong urging of Theodore Roosevelt, announced his nomination of Wood to be chief of staff, the change to take effect the following March. This nomination met no resistance in Congress. The regular officers of the Army had now accepted Wood as one of their own, impressed by the way he had accepted full personal responsibility for the much–criticized Mount Dajo massacre in 1906.

But Wood had a problem: his appointment would be contingent on his passing a medical exam. In general his health was excellent, but he still suffered from the head injury he had incurred back in 1899 at Santiago. Although a surgical operation in 1905 had relieved his symptoms to a large degree, the paralysis of his left side, which he had always been able to hide, had reappeared. He was also subject to seizures. He could usually forestall those episodes by the use of a handkerchief and a small bottle of chloroform, but that device was now beginning to lose its effectiveness.

In February 1909, Wood had made contact, under a social pretext, with a brilliant young neurosurgeon from Johns Hopkins Medical Center named Harvey Cushing. Cushing wanted to perform an exploratory operation at that time, but he had not yet reached the prominence he would later attain, and two influential surgeons had overridden his judgment. Wood had agreed. But now, a year later, with the prospect of being disqualified for a position he craved, Wood approached Cushing again. The doctor operated on him on February 5, 1910.

The procedure was extremely complicated, and Wood's loss of blood was so severe that Cushing did not complete it on the first try. A second effort, a few days later, was more satisfactory, and Cushing believed that he had successfully removed the entire tumor. Wood's rapid recovery, due partly to his otherwise superb physical condition, reinforced the doctor's belief. By March 5, 1910, only a month after entering the hospital, Wood was back at work at his office on Governors Island. His nomination confirmed, he was set to assume the most important role of his career, that of chief of staff of the United States Army.

The army of which Wood became the uniformed chief on July 19, 1910, was in a bad condition. The drastic paper reorganization that Elihu Root had engineered in 1902 had created an excellent framework, but putting its provisions on the books and forcing compliance were two different things. In addition, the Army was still undermanned, undersupplied, and ill–directed. Appropriations were so tightly controlled by Congress that most of the staff felt powerless. Paperwork was so voluminous that one seven–page memo signed by both Bell and Secretary of War Jacob M. Dickinson had ended, "It is therefore recommended that no toilet paper be issued."[3]

Wood lost no time in reorganizing the staff. He divided it into four divisions: mobile army, coast artillery, militia affairs, and the War College. Each division was to be headed by an assistant chief of staff, and paperwork was to be reduced drastically. In his report for 1911, the new secretary of war, Harry L. Stimson, estimated that Wood's reforms had saved the Army $245,000 in paperwork alone.[4]

The Army's effectiveness was further crippled by the fact that its units were scattered among about fifty posts, most of them relics from the days of the Indian Wars. Their sole function was now to bring federal money into various congressional districts. The representatives of those districts regarded every small post as sacrosanct. Given that obstacle, Wood could only begin the job; in fact, he finally had to admit defeat. The failure embarrassed him and, worse, made any effort to concentrate a force much more difficult.

In early 1911, an emergency arose that temporarily assisted Wood's efforts. It was brought about by a new and unexpected unrest in Mexico, where much of the population of the northern Mexican states was rising against the aging and autocratic dictator, Porfirio Díaz. For many years, American troops along the long common border had been dangerously spread out, justified only by the fact that Díaz, a friend of American business, had kept the situation stable. But Díaz had lost support, and he obviously had stolen the presidential election of 1910. A large portion of the country was now rallying behind a rebellion led by Francisco Madero, a wealthy Coahuila landowner. Groups of rebels were beginning to gather, and defecting Mexican troops were crossing the border, especially into Texas. By February 1911, when Madero's forces took the city of Juarez, across the Rio Grande from El Paso, Díaz was obviously doomed. Wood, alarmed by the chaos, sought a meeting with President Taft, asking permission to concentrate American troops along the border and possibly create a buffer zone across the Rio Grande. Taft instructed him to alert the forces in Texas but to go no further.

3. Wood to M. Y. Bunyan Varillas, August 17, 1910, Wood Papers, cited in McCallum, *Leonard Wood,* 242.

4. McCallum, *Leonard Wood,* 242.

A couple of weeks later, however, Taft had for some reason decided to take limited action. On March 6, 1911, he ordered Wood to concentrate as many troops as possible along the border. Wood was elated but realized that he now faced a major operation, as many of the posts the troops would come from held only a company of troops. But Wood was happy about one thing: four of his subordinate generals, who had never commanded formations of even regimental size, would gain experience. Because Taft desired to conceal the purpose of the concentration, the troops were to proceed to San Antonio "for maneuvers." This professed purpose, transparent as it was, resulted in the name "Maneuver Division."

It took Wood and his staff three months to assemble twenty thousand troops at Fort Sam Houston, San Antonio, and when they arrived they did not present an impressive sight. Most of the regiments were at half strength; the officers were below standard, and half of the troops were utterly green. So ragged was the division that Wood was embarrassed when foreign observers were around. Fortunately for Wood and his staff, however, Taft was delighted with even this sorry show of force, and after the concentration had been under way for about ten days he expressed his happiness at how things had gone.

At the same time, Taft gave Wood a set of very difficult instructions. No American troops were to cross the border, even in hot pursuit. Wood must be careful to avoid offending the touchy Texans, whose territory was being occupied by federal troops for the first time since Reconstruction. Wood made the best use of his time by instituting a training program.

By August, when the fighting in Mexico began moving farther south, the Maneuver Division was abandoned. By Taft's specification, the entire exercise had been performed within the Army's normal budget. Many other observers besides Taft hailed this temporary concentration as an achievement. But to Wood, who had witnessed military maneuvers of French and Germans on two visits to Europe, American weakness was alarming.

One of Wood's greatest accomplishments in his four years as chief of staff was to put teeth into the reorganization of the Army staff that had been accomplished by Secretary of War Elihu Root (under Theodore Roosevelt) in 1902. Inertia—the old way of doing things—still ruled. The first three chiefs of staff to serve after the "reorganization" had felt no need to rock the boat.[5] The result was that the technical services—adjutant general, engineers, quartermaster, and so forth—continued to conduct business as usual. Of these,

5. Samuel Young, Adna Chaffee, and John Bates.

the adjutant general had been able to keep his unofficial status as the "most important officer in the Army." The other technical services were also entrenched, but those bureaucrats were discreet in their exercise of power, and each governed only one phase of Army activities. The adjutant general was the center of the feud.

The adjutant general at the time Wood took office as chief of staff was Major General Fred Ainsworth, by coincidence an officer who had also come into the Army as a doctor. Ainsworth was one of Wood's oldest acquaintances, stemming from their days together as contract surgeons chasing Apache back in 1886. But their subsequent paths to power had been different. Wood had risen to his position on the basis of duty in combat. Ainsworth had arrived by dint of becoming the most consummate bureaucrat in the Army. Ainsworth was charming, handsome, adroit, and an expert at manipulating Congress. He would be a formidable rival.

The two men started out working together on cordial terms. When Wood arrived in Washington from New York, he stayed as a guest at Ainsworth's home. They breakfasted together at least a couple of times. At their offices in the old State–War–Navy Building across from the White House, they bent over backward to show courtesy to each other. They hand–carried papers back and forth, and Wood made a point of going over to the adjutant general's office when they had business, instead of sending for him. But all this excessive courtesy was artificial; the two ambitious men were only feeling each other out.

Finally, Wood made one gesture to show independence. When he replaced officers with new ones in his drastic overhaul of the Army staff, he made sure to appoint at least some men other than those that Ainsworth had recommended. The honeymoon was nearing its end.

The difficulties between Wood and Ainsworth, aside from the determination of each to be the top dog, were long term and short term. The long–term difficulty was one of background, the fact that Wood represented the "progressive" element in the Army, whereas Ainsworth represented the status quo. He had spent twenty years in the War Department ensuring that he could control everything at his fingertips. Only one door led from the hallway into the office of the adjutant general; all the others bore a sign, "No Admittance." Everyone wanting to do business had to go through him.

Predictably, Ainsworth detested the idea of a general staff, and before Wood arrived he had been so effective in frustrating Wood's predecessors that Chaffee had become embittered and Bell had actually wound up in the hospital. Wood, however, was a tougher infighter, and he could stand up with coolness to Ainsworth's allies in the Congress. This group included Congressman

James Hay of Virginia, the chairman of the House Committee on Military Affairs, and the still influential Senator Francis Warren of Wyoming.

Wood, however, was supported by even heavier artillery: Secretary of War Dickinson and to a lesser degree President Taft himself. In May 1911, Wood's alliance was strengthened when Henry L. Stimson became secretary of war, a man even more zealous about strengthening the General Staff and supporting Wood than Dickinson.

The immediate trigger for the open break between Wood and Ainsworth was the seemingly minor issue of paperwork, which Wood had been working to reduce from the day he took office. On Wood's recommendation, Secretary Stimson appointed a board of officers to study the problem. It was chaired by Ainsworth, the "goat to guard the cabbage." Ainsworth was undoubtedly aware that the bulk of the board members would be against him, and accordingly saw to it that the studies of the committee went along at a snail's pace.

The break came into the open for the first time when the report was due a year later. In the meantime, Ainsworth confronted Wood, claiming that his office was not being allowed to exert the "proper influence in the Department." Here was Wood's chance: he shot back that he intended to treat the adjutant general's office as he would any other bureau of the War Department. That direct challenge brought a complete end to any surface appearance of cordiality between the two men.[6]

A seemingly unimportant issue dealt with the length of the individual soldier's enlistment. Ainsworth visualized a professional regular army, characterized by long enlistments—five years. Wood, on the other hand, advocated a ten–year enlistment, of which only the first two years would be spent on active duty, with the last eight years spent in the highly trained reserves. The longer regular enlistments, as Wood saw it, would result in a man's signing up every five years, making a lifetime career as a professional private, few in number. Such an army would be adequate only for the very limited missions that Ainsworth envisioned for the nation's defense needs. Wood, who expected a major war, wanted to vastly expand the Army. To do that, he sought to create a pool of trained civilians, ready to enter active service with minimum training. He could, he claimed, train a private in a mere six months.

It was not a difference in concept, however, that brought about Ainsworth's downfall; it was his refusal even to consider any War Department procedures that differed from his own. When the board of officers set up to study Army procedures and paperwork completed its report, Ainsworth disapproved of

6. Hagedorn, *Leonard Wood, a Biography,* 2:108.

its findings. His personal recommendations were challenged at the last minute by the recorder. Ainsworth was able to muster the votes to override the rebel, but the minority findings reached Stimson and Wood, who accepted them over the official ones. Wood sent his conclusion (and Stimson's) to Ainsworth for comment.

Ainsworth refused to cooperate. He sat on Wood's request for three weeks, and when Wood nudged him he again withheld comment. Three weeks later, Wood sent him an ultimatum: "with the least practicable delay."[7]

At that point, Ainsworth broke. His response was vitriolic, full of remarks directed toward Wood, Stimson, and even Taft, using such terms as *uninformed, subterfuge,* and *incompetent amateurs.* One look at the document showed Wood that he had won: Ainsworth's terminology exceeded the bounds of insubordination. He took the paper to Stimson.

Stimson now took personal charge of the matter. He showed the document to President Taft and Elihu Root, who was now a senator from New York, and the Army's judge advocate general. The issue was reduced to a decision of whether to deal with Ainsworth administratively, issuing only a reprimand, or to prefer charges for court–martial. All agreed with Stimson's pleas for a court–martial. The secretary wasted no time in preparing the necessary papers and within hours relieved Ainsworth of his position. Ainsworth was to go home and await the proceedings.

The day after Stimson had taken this action, President Taft was called out of a cabinet meeting by request of Senator Warren, who had come to the White House on "urgent business." As Ainsworth's strongest supporter, Warren had come on his friend's behalf, requesting permission for him to retire from the Army rather than face a court–martial. Taft returned to the cabinet meeting chuckling. When he told the cabinet members what had transpired, everyone, Stimson in particular, agreed. Granting permission to retire would be the best way out of a difficult situation. The president approved. Many, including Stimson and some of Ainsworth's friends, were surprised that Ainsworth, a man they considered a formidable fighter, had elected not to contest the matter to the bitter end. But Ainsworth was wise. He realized that he had no defense for the intemperate language he had used, and he left quietly.[8]

Wood's troubles did not end there. Senator Warren and Representative Hay attempted to exact revenge by introducing a rider to an all–important defense appropriations bill that would have made Wood ineligible to be

7. Ibid., 120–21.

8. Harry L. Stimson and McGeorge Bundy, *On Active Service in Peace and War,* 33–37.

chief of staff. The rider specified that a chief of staff must have served in a line position below that of general officer for ten years. The provision would have made Wood ineligible for his present position, but it was manifestly ridiculous; it would have done the same to almost any other head of the Army in US history. Taft, despite the urgency of defense appropriations, and beset on the political front, had the courage to veto the bill. Matters were soon worked out.

The relief that Wood and Stimson felt to have the Ainsworth matter settled was diluted, unfortunately, by a decision on the part of their mutual friend, Theodore Roosevelt. Dissatisfied with Taft, and longing for power, the former president had decided to challenge Taft for the Republican presidential nomination in 1912. The news hit both Wood and Stimson hard. Wood was Roosevelt's close personal friend; Stimson was Roosevelt's protégé. But both men were also serving the incumbent president, and by any accounting they owed Taft their loyalty.

Wood's position was easier than Stimson's. As a professional Army officer, he was expected to avoid anything resembling partisan politics, a policy to which he had always adhered. He was therefore able to remain quiet. It was well that he could do so, because with Roosevelt's rash decision there could be no pleasing him.

Stimson enjoyed no such privilege—or believed that he did not. As a political appointee of President Taft, and therefore part of the administration, he felt himself obligated to speak out on the current president's behalf. But first he tried to avoid the break by urging Roosevelt to desist from his challenge. In early January, Stimson and Secretary of the Navy George von L. Meyer visited Roosevelt at Oyster Bay. The atmosphere was friendly, even warm, and Stimson left feeling some hope. By the end of the month, however, just as the Ainsworth affair was closing down, Roosevelt threw his hat in the ring.

Nothing good could come from this situation, not for Taft, not for the Republicans, and not for Roosevelt. The rest of the story has often been told. Taft was able to retain the Republican nomination when it met at Chicago in June, but the split made the election of Woodrow Wilson, governor of New Jersey, inevitable. Roosevelt's Bull Moose Party, as he called it, polled more votes than did Taft, but both were short of the votes garnered by Wilson.

In the few months remaining of the Taft administration, Stimson and Wood were able to put the finishing touches on Army reorganization. Although they could not secure congressional approval to reduce the number of posts, they could at least reorganize them. They divided the continental United States into four regions and organized each as a division. A given "division" would have its proportional allotment of infantry, artillery, cavalry, and engineers. Each would be commanded by a brigadier general. In case of need, a single division could be mobilized, even though its components were widely scattered. In the War Department, the General Staff organization would admittedly remain fragile. Wood and Stimson had done all they could.

Stimson left his office, along with all the other members of the Taft administration, on March 4, 1913, and in the months of interregnum it was not certain that President–elect Woodrow Wilson would retain Wood as Army chief of staff. As a general rule, a chief of staff is appointed for a four–year term independent of the administration in power. But legally, the chief of staff serves "at the pleasure of the president." If Wilson so desired, he could replace Wood at will.

There were reasons Wilson might exercise that option. Animosity against Wood still prevailed in some quarters—Senator Warren and Congressman Hay had seen to that—and Wilson, by nature a pacifist, was doubtless aware of Wood's proclivities toward imperialism. Besides, as governor of New Jersey, Wilson had cleaned house when he had taken over there. And finally, of course, Wood's friendship with Theodore Roosevelt was common knowledge, a fact that could hardly work to Wood's advantage.

Wood, however, had staunch allies. The bulk of the Army officer corps sided enthusiastically with him against the now–defunct Ainsworth group, the main source of Warren's enmity. And General Hugh Scott, currently superintendent at West Point, parlayed a visit to his brother, a Princeton man and a friend of Wilson's, to see Wilson himself. Wilson, as governor of New Jersey, was not provided with living quarters, and he was still residing in the town. Scott was a genial, persuasive man, and he explained the Army's view to the governor. He left encouraged, and doubtless had been able to exert some influence. But Wood's case was also pleaded by Wilson's close adviser, Colonel Edward House, and House's attitude was probably responsible for Wood's retention in office until the end of his four–year term.

Although Wood was aggrieved to see the Republican Party ousted from the presidency, he felt himself fortunate to discover that the new secretary of war, Lindley Garrison, was a man in the mold of Wood's two former superiors, Dickinson and Stimson. Like his predecessors, Garrison was a successful lawyer. He was forty–six years old at the time, energetic, interested in the Army, and not afraid to use American power in situations where it was called for. He had been, like many of the rest of President Wilson's cabinet, selected almost whimsically, having come to the attention of Governor Wilson in New Jersey. Garrison was one of the stronger of Wilson's first cabinet.

The first foreign crisis that Wilson faced on assuming office involved another phase of the fighting in Mexico, where President Francisco Madero, who had ousted Porfirio Díaz as president in early 1911, had proved inept as a revolutionary leader. Among Madero's failings was an idealistic belief in the goodness of his associates, and he left men in office who not only wished him ill but took positive steps to destroy him. Foremost among these was General Victoriano Huerta, head of the Mexican Army and a personal friend of the deposed Díaz. From the start, Huerta began plotting against Madero, and by February 1913 he had replaced him as president.

Huerta's usurpation of power might have been accepted had it not been dramatized by murder. On February 22, ten days before the Wilson inauguration, Madero was secretly removed from his prison cell in the National Palace of Mexico City, taken a few blocks across the city to another prison, and shot dead. No definite proof has ever linked Huerta with the event, but the circumstantial evidence is strong that he at least approved. The two assassins, one a corporal, were soon promoted to the grade of general with no protest from Huerta.

This episode in Mexico, though of no official concern to the United States, put Woodrow Wilson in a state of upset. Convinced that Huerta had seized office illegally and had engineered Madero's death, the idealistic Wilson refused to recognize the Huerta regime while at the same time declaring that the United States would stay out of Mexico's internal affairs. He sent emissaries to Mexico, men who did not even speak the language. Their missions not only were of no value, but caused enough resentment among the Mexicans as to be positively harmful.

The diplomatic decisions, or lack thereof, affected Garrison and Wood only indirectly. Wood, as always suspicious of Japanese intentions, had received surreptitious reports of Japanese plans to build a base in Baja California, Mexico. He therefore pleaded for more troops and drafted plans to defeat a possible Japanese invasion of Mexico. He submitted his plans to President Wilson. Wilson, however, was conscious of appearing to harbor any sort of aggressive intentions, and he refused to consider increasing the strength of the Army. In addition, he ordered the suspension of any further planning. There the matter stood, in limbo, throughout the winter of 1913–14.

In Mexico, meanwhile, rebellions once more arose, this time against Huerta. The two most important, as usual, began in the northern Mexican states where Governor Venustiano Carranza in Coahuila and Francisco (Pancho) Villa in Sonora, both former Madero men, launched parallel revolutions. At this point, President Wilson made a decision that was to have far-reaching effects: he lifted Taft's ban on the sale of arms to the rebels, assuming that his currently cordial relations with Carranza would remain permanent. Munitions began pouring across the border from the United States into northern Mexico. Garrison and Wood were disturbed; even the employees of the Remington Company in New England, people whose personal financial gain was involved, disliked the sale. But the decision came from the president himself.

In April 1914, a strange crisis occurred. At Tampico, on the Gulf of Mexico, a boat belonging to the US naval squadron was seized by a zealous Mexican colonel but quickly released with an apology. That, however, failed to satisfy the local admiral, who considered the incident an insult to the American flag and demanded excessive apologies. After much confusion, word reached the White House. Wilson called a meeting, and eventually the Atlantic Fleet occupied Veracruz, the principal Mexican seaport. American troops remained for several months—all this without a declaration of war.

Wood and Garrison were both present at the crucial meeting but had little or nothing to contribute. However, in this time of tension, Wood was permitted to send a cavalry brigade under the command of General Pershing from the Presidio of California to El Paso. He was also allowed to deploy numerous National Guard units along the border. Although the guardsmen never fired a shot, they began to develop some organization, a move that would be of value in the future.

In spite of all this furor, Wood was able to accomplish a project that would lead to his greatest contribution to military preparedness: the beginning of a reserve system. He began, with Garrison's (and Roosevelt's) encouragement, to preach the idea in the various universities of the obligation of America's elite to take the lead in national service. The idea came from an unusual source. A young lieutenant, Henry T. Bull, assigned as a military science professor[9] at Cornell University, had read of a Navy scheme for taking college students aboard ship for two-month cruises. Bull became convinced that the Army could do the same, and he made a special trip to Washington to present the idea to Wood in person. Wood snapped the idea up and assigned two young officers, one of whom was Douglas MacArthur, to draw up plans. Garrison supported the idea and found the funds to make the program possible.

In early-May 1913, Wood sent a circular letter to various college presidents, saying that the secretary of war was establishing two summer training camps

9. Professor of military science and tactics (PMS&T), a standard assignment.

for young college men, the purpose of which would be to "increase the present inadequate personnel of the trained military reserve of the United States." He assured the university presidents that the object was not one of military aggrandizement, but a means of "meeting a vital need confronting a peaceful, unmilitary, though warlike nation . . . by a more thorough preparation . . . to resist any effort to break such peace."[10] Wood's wording may have been vague, but the idea was warmly received, and during the summer Wood established two camps, one at Gettysburg, Pennsylvania, and the other at Monterey, California. During the summer of 1913, 159 students, each paying his own expenses, went through the Gettysburg camp; 63 attended at Monterey.[11]

The results were astonishing, especially to the Army officers running the camps. Accustomed to training relatively uneducated young men in the Regular Army, they were not prepared for the speed with which their new charges learned military techniques, sanitation, and long–distance marches. Their enthusiasm was also remarkable. And one of the benefits was the salutary effect that enthusiasm had on the college presidents, who responded as well.

Wood contributed personally. Though quiet and sometimes ruthless, he was capable of great charm. His attitude was contagious, and even such pacifists as Nicholas Murray Butler of Columbia and David Starr Jordan of Stanford supported the program.[12]

Of all the college presidents, the most enthusiastic was the dignified, white–haired Henry Sturgis Drinker, of Lehigh University. Not only did Drinker's son attend, but he himself spent the first training session in person, living in the tent with the trainees and participating in what activities he could. At the Century Club in New York, Drinker organized the Advisory Board of University Presidents for the National Reserve Corps, with John Hibben of Princeton as chairman. Eight college presidents constituted the board.[13]

The seeds of the Plattsburg training camp had been planted. Wood had begun the Army Reserve Program, which would be so vital to the US war effort in 1917.

Wood's tour as chief of staff of the Army ended on April 12, 1914, about four months before the outbreak of war in Europe.[14] On his departure, Wood

10. John Garry Clifford, *The Citizen Soldiers: The Plattsburg Training Camp Movement, 1913–1920,* 11–12.

11. Hagedorn, *Leonard Wood, a Biography,* 2:132.

12. Clifford, *Citizen Soldiers,* 18–19.

13. Ibid., 21–22.

14. He was succeeded by Major General William W. Wotherspoon, who served only seven months before mandatory retirement age. Wotherspoon was followed by Wood's friend and colleague Hugh Scott.

received a letter of appreciation from President Wilson, expressing sentiments that the president probably did not wholly feel. By custom, Wood could have retired from the Army, as did most officers leaving the post. But because he was only fifty–four years old, with ten years of service left ahead of him, he remained on active duty. To his satisfaction, he was assigned once more to the Eastern Department, where the bulk of America's combat troops were located.

Before he left Washington, however, Wood had another important job to perform. Plans were afoot to organize a field army as part of the Eastern Department, and presumably Wood would command it personally. Planning for it kept Wood in communication with the whole Army, and in the process he received two remarkable letters. One came from Brigadier General John J. Pershing, asking for assignment to a cavalry brigade at El Paso, Texas. Relations between Mexico and the United States were tense, due to the sequence of events at Tampico that culminated in American occupation of Veracruz. War had not been declared, though Wilson's actions could be considered justification. Fighting might break out in several places, the most likely at El Paso.[15] Pershing's letter, surprising in light of his lukewarm regard for Wood, bordered on the obsequious. In it he offered, in case of hostilities, to serve in an infantry or a cavalry brigade under Wood himself, offering to serve as his chief of staff. Wood assigned Pershing to command at El Paso, as requested.[16]

An even more remarkable letter came from Major Douglas MacArthur, currently serving with Brigadier General Frederick Funston at Veracruz. "General Funston," MacArthur began, "is handling things very well and there is room for little criticism, but I miss the inspiration, my dear General, of your own cleaner, decisive methods. I hope sincerely affairs shape themselves so that you will shortly take the field for the campaign, which, if death does not call you, can have but one ending—The White House."[17]

MacArthur was only a major at the time, and the letter showed amazing temerity in comparing the performance of one general officer with that of another. But MacArthur, a shrewd man, would never mention such an idea as a Wood presidency had he not been certain that the idea would be well received.

Returning to field duty could not help having an appeal to Wood, but he had another incentive for staying in service: he had adopted military

15. The commander at Veracruz, who had relieved the Navy and Marine Corps that had first occupied it, was Brigadier General Frederick Funston, the man who had captured Aguinaldo and was considered to be the foremost combat leader in the Army.

16. Hagedorn, *Leonard Wood, a Biography,* 2:147.

17. MacArthur to Wood, May 7, 1914, cited in ibid.

preparedness for war as his main obsession. He was not the Anglophile that other future members of the "Preparedness Movement" were—men such as Roosevelt, Root, and Stimson—but he was well aware of American weakness, and on his arrival at Governors Island on July 10, 1914, he set out to make the United States capable of defense against any power, not ruling out even Britain.

15

The Sinking of the *Lusitania*

Theodore Roosevelt was a man who held strong likes and dislikes, and one of his dislikes was Woodrow Wilson. Their personalities were at the ends of the pole—the man of action versus the intellectual. But the difference in personality was not the cause for animosity; it was Wilson's habit of throwing cold water on just about all of Roosevelt's proud achievements. Like other Democrats, Wilson had strongly opposed American occupation of the Philippines, and they protested when Roosevelt, as president, established American ownership of the islands when he signed the treaty with Emilio Aguinaldo in 1902. Worse, Wilson had also loftily disapproved of Roosevelt's role in encouraging the Panamanian breakaway from Colombia, in order to enable the United States to build the Panama Canal. Wilson had, in fact, apologized to Colombia and had paid the large sum of twenty–five million dollars in reparations.[1]

On one issue, however, Roosevelt would be on Wilson's side when the then president declared a policy of strict neutrality when the European war broke out in early–August 1914. Roosevelt viewed the British blockade of Germany as equally distasteful as the highly publicized (and exaggerated) German atrocities in Belgium.

Roosevelt had another, though minor, reason for neutrality. Like Wood, he had developed a sort of kinship with Kaiser Wilhelm II. He was, however, careful not to be used in that regard. When the kaiser sent him a message

1. There were other complaints. Wilson had acceded to British demands that American ships pay tolls, even when crossing the Panama Canal from one American port to another.

reminding him of their former meetings and appealing for understanding, he answered courteously in his reply, but added favorable remarks about King Albert of Belgium in the same sentence. Although Roosevelt admired certain aspects of German and Japanese culture, the main basis of his praise was directed at their strong national defenses. There he found Wilson and Secretary of State William Jennings Bryan most at fault.[2]

Except for the encouragement from fellow preparedness enthusiasts such as Roosevelt, Stimson, and Root, Wood was alone in pursuing his purposes within the governmental establishment. Despite the hellish summer of 1914 in Europe, culminating with the outbreak of war, grim stories of the German invasion of Belgium, and the dramatic Battle of the Marne, the attitude of both the people and the government was remarkably complacent. War, or at least American participation in war, was "unthinkable." Wilson and the public thought that US participation was remote as of the end of 1914. Early the next year, the complacency was to be dispelled.

On May 1, 1915, the Royal Merchant Ship *Lusitania* set sail from New York Harbor, bound for Liverpool on what was planned as a six–day voyage. Its sailing did not go unnoticed; in fact, it was a major event. Passenger crossings of the Atlantic were rare in this ninth month of the European war, because most of Britain's merchant fleet of prewar years had been pressed into service as troopships, hospitals, and cargo vessels. Besides, the *Lusitania,* named after the ancient Roman name for Portugal, was no ordinary liner. It and its sister ship, the *Mauretania,* were the fastest vessels afloat, with top speeds of more than twenty–six knots. They were both built in 1907, and at that time had been the largest passenger ships afloat. Granted, the Cunard Line had subsequently built the larger *Olympia,* but this new rival could not match the speed of the *Lusitania.* Besides, the *Olympia* and the *Mauretania* had both been drafted into duty. The *Lusitania* was almost the only British passenger ship in service.

Unfortunately, the military status of the *Lusitania* was vague. Because the Cunard Line had needed governmental help in constructing it, the company had gone to the British Admiralty for financial assistance. The assistance had been granted, but to justify the expenditure the Admiralty had required that it be listed as an alternative cruiser of the Royal Navy, available for use in time of war. Mounts for guns were welded into the decks. Furthermore, the cargo manifest for this crossing included forty–two hundred cases of rifle cartridges

2. Brands, *T. R.*, 751.

and twelve hundred cases of shell casings, all open for public scrutiny. The ship was forbidden by vague agreements with Germany that no war materials should be carried aboard passenger vessels, but in the British view the restriction did not include small–arms ammunition. The *Lusitania* was not carrying the main contraband—artillery ammunition, shells, and powder.

The *Lusitania,* therefore, was known to be at some risk in making this voyage. The danger in the crossing came from the threat of German submarines, used because the German surface navy had essentially been swept from the seas. In the days of the surface ships, it had been possible, when a warship was about to sink an enemy merchant vessel, to give warning ahead of time to allow the passengers to abandon ship. But the U–boat was slower than a surface ship, and its very survival depended on stealth. The humanitarian act of warning was therefore now a thing of the past. In addition, the German government, on February 4, 1915, had declared the seas around the British Isles to be a war zone, effective from the eighteenth on. British and French ships in the area would be sunk without warning. Germany would attempt to spare neutral shipping, but identifying it as such might not always be possible.

At the same time, Germany was anxious to keep the United States out of the war, though it was well known that American munitions companies were conducting a profitable trade with Britain, especially in artillery ammunition. But trade was one thing, and the risk to lives was another. On April 22, therefore, the German Embassy in Washington issued a warning that was carried in some fifty American newspapers:

> TRAVELLERS intending to embark on the Atlantic voyage are reminded that a state of war exists between Germany and her allies and Great Britain and her allies; that the zone of war includes the waters adjacent to the British Isles; that, in accordance with formal notice given by the Imperial German Government, vessels carrying the flag of Great Britain, or any of her allies, are liable to destruction in those waters and that travellers sailing in the war zone on ships of Great Britain or her allies do so at their own risk.
>
> IMPERIAL GERMAN EMBASSY
> Washington, D.C. 22d April 1915

Despite that warning, 139 Americans took the risk and sailed.

On April 30, 1915, the day before the *Lusitania* sailed from New York, the German U–boat *U–20,* commanded by Captain Walther Schwieger,[3] left the

3. Schwieger's actual rank was lieutenant, but he was captain of the ship.

German port of Borkum, headed for the Irish Sea. To avoid the dangers of travel through the English Channel, Schwieger sailed north of Scotland and down the west coast of Ireland. Although British intelligence had discovered the path of the *U–20,* that agency had not disseminated its findings to the fleet. Protection of the secret means of acquiring the German messages was so closely held that the word never left the offices of the higher admirals.

Then followed a series of errors that add up to an ironic story. On May 5, the *U–20* sank a British schooner, *The Earl of Lathom,* and the next day it sank several other ships. When Captain William Turner, commanding the *Lusitania,* was notified that evening that German submarines were in his area, there was little that he could do. He ordered the usual precautions such as locking the compartmental doors, posting double guards, and putting the ship under blackout. He then went about normal activities.

The next day, the *U–20* was low on supplies and down to three torpedoes. Satisfied with the success of his mission, Captain Schwieger had decided to return to Germany when all of a sudden he spotted a large ship coming out of the fog at a point about ten miles south of Kinsale, Ireland. At first Schwieger thought he had encountered a group of ships, but he soon realized that the four stacks without doubt identified the *Lusitania.* For some reason, he tailed the ship, which was going at slow speed because of the fog, and then fired a single torpedo, saw it hit the ship, causing two explosions, and then departed the scene.[4] Captain Turner immediately gave the order to abandon ship. The vessel sank in eighteen minutes, the death rate being multiplied by the inability of passengers and crew to move through the locked compartments. Of the forty–eight lifeboats aboard the ship, only six functioned. Turner went down with his ship but survived to spend the rest of his life testifying and reliving that awful moment of 2:10 p.m., May 7, 1915.

Out of 1,959 people aboard, 1,198 died. Of the Americans, only 9 of the 139 survived.

The German government announced the sinking the day after it occurred, pointing out that the *Lusitania* had been carrying contraband of

4. Immediately after the sinking of the *Lusitania,* several investigations were launched in Britain to ascertain responsibility for the disaster. The British government, interested primarily in fixing responsibility, focused its investigation on the actions of Captain Turner. The case was difficult to make because of the flurries of messages that had been sent to him in the hours preceding the attack. The Cunard Line, however, had a concern of its own. In order to show the ship construction in the best light, the company found witnesses to attest that the *Lusitania* had been sunk by two torpedoes, not just one. To back up that claim, they pointed to the second explosion, contested by nobody. Captain Turner's

war and was classed as an "auxiliary cruiser" in the Royal Navy. The announcement also cited the note issued by the German Embassy that took effect on February 18, 1915, warning civilians that they were sailing in the war zone at their own risk.

Despite those arguments of the Germans, the American public reaction was one of outrage. Captain Schwieger was declared a "war criminal" in the press. Because many of the victims of the sinking had been New Yorkers, the *New York Times* featured the sinking for more than a week and even in the Great War that followed two years later reminded the public in every week's rotogravure of the victims. The public furor lasted only about a week, however. There was too much other news to absorb the public's interest. The *Washington Times,*[5] for example, reported the current Russian drive against Warsaw on the German eastern front with greater emphasis than that given the *Lusitania.* That issue did, however, give a dire headline warning: "America Faces Growing Peril of War as the Result of Germany's Policy of Submarine Warfare." Never mind that America's entry into the war would be nearly two years off. The sinking of the *Lusitania* cost Germany its support in the United States and other countries. From now on, America would be "neutral on the side of Britain and France."

The episode caused splits in the Wilson administration. It triggered a growing rift between President Woodrow Wilson and his secretary of state, William Jennings Bryan, who soon resigned over what he considered too strong a reaction on Wilson's part.

On May 13, six days after the sinking, Wilson made a statement reaffirming the rights of American citizens to travel on merchant ships and called on the Germans to cease attacks on merchant vessels. Three weeks later, on June 9, the president was more specific. He rejected the German claim that the British blockade of German ports was illegal, as the Germans claimed. He also claimed, with dubious accuracy, that the *Lusitania* had not been carrying illegal arms. Later, Wilson went so far as to issue an ultimatum to the effect that any subsequent sinkings would be regarded by the United States as "deliberately unfriendly." All this was too belligerent for Bryan, and he resigned his

---

first report had described only one torpedo, striking the ship between the third and fourth smokestacks. Later, under pressure, he changed his testimony to attest that his ship had been hit by two torpedoes. Later, the pressure off, he reverted to his earlier position of a single missile. Eventually, the findings exonerated everyone—the British Admiralty, the Cunard Line, and Turner.

5. The *Washington Times* was a newspaper that existed between 1902 and 1929, not to be confused with the paper of a later date.

post. He was replaced by his undersecretary, Robert Lansing, a man considerably more friendly to the British cause and less pacifistic in his views.

Yet Wilson was by no means ready to go to war over the sinking of a British vessel carrying American passengers. He stood by an oddly worded statement he had made in Philadelphia on May 10, just after the tragedy, designed to allay the concerns of ethnic Americans that he was being too truculent: "There is such a thing as a man being too proud to fight. There is such a thing as a nation being so right that it does not need to convince others by force that it is right." The words *too proud to fight* may have reassured frightened Americans, but they infuriated Theodore Roosevelt. His previous advice that the United States should stay out of the European war was never repeated. He and his cohorts were now convinced that the United States should enter the war on the side of Britain and France as soon as possible.

16

The Buildup Starts

The sinking of the *Lusitania* came as less of a surprise to Wood than to most Americans, because, unlike his countrymen, he had long been convinced that war was coming. Nevertheless, it did not change his status.

Roosevelt, on the other hand, was aroused, so much so that he resurrected his dream of raising a volunteer division, as he had back in 1911. He saw himself commanding an enlarged version of the Rough Riders of nearly twenty years earlier.[1] No such epiphany seems to have struck Wood.

The *Lusitania* tragedy did, however, encourage the proponents of preparedness, and for once the issue was not in the realm of partisan politics. Colonel Edward House, Secretary of War Lindley Garrison, and Assistant Secretary of the Navy Franklin Roosevelt were Democrats; Senator Elihu Root, Henry Stimson, and Senator Henry Cabot Lodge were Republicans, all working together. True, many Republicans tended to interpret Woodrow Wilson's reluctance as unpatriotic, and to ward off this tendency Secretary Garrison had seen fit to warn his political opponents openly against that. But as of May 1915, that danger had temporarily disappeared, and President Wilson was beginning to see the sway of public opinion and was becoming a bit less cautious.

The Preparedness Movement was well financed and prestigious. Ironically, however, their cause of advocating an increase in Army strength was damaged, not aided, by the fact that war was raging in Europe. Armies cost money, and at that time, in the absence of a federal income tax, government

1. John Patrick Finnegan, *Against the Specter of a Dragon: The Campaign for American Military Preparedness, 1914–1917*, 38.

revenue came from the tariff. With European commerce curtailed by the British naval blockade of Germany and Germany's U–boat menace, tariff rates had to go up.

Most of these considerations fell outside of Leonard Wood's purview. The idea of restricting his activities to military affairs, however, had never been one of his outstanding traits. In the year after returning to Governors Island, he made an estimated sixty speeches preaching his gospel of military preparedness, even though he was skirting the line of propriety. A congressman once described him as "the most aggressive and most persistent officer who was ever Chief of Staff, in my memory. . . . Whatever may be his merits or demerits, he was a man who had the courage of his convictions and who never lost an opportunity in expressing those views."[2] The congressman's views were widely shared by those who came in contact with Leonard Wood.

One of Wood's critics was Secretary of War Lindley Garrison, not his direct boss. In advocating military preparedness, they were allies, but they indulged in a mutual dislike. This contrasted dramatically with the friendship Wood had enjoyed with Secretary Henry Stimson, whose admiration for him had been unbounded. The fact is they were rivals. Garrison was an authoritarian who wanted all relations between the Army and the public to be handled by his own office. Wood, however, spoke to audiences with authority, not in the name of Garrison. This state of affairs did not, however, materially affect their mutual dedication to the cause of preparedness.

Wood possessed one distinct advantage in his rivalry with Garrison: his responsibilities in the Eastern Department were sufficiently limited that he had time to concentrate on one issue, preaching preparedness. He sought and attained allies, and he got them in men outside of government. One of these was a wealthy, well–connected young lawyer named Grenville Clark, a Harvard graduate and a member of Elihu Root's law firm. Clark assisted Wood in drawing members of the university elite into service. He and Wood were convinced that the priority lay in developing an officer corps and that a major source of officers should be the graduates of America's universities. To that end, Clark founded the Committee of One Hundred, consisting of Ivy League graduates, who met periodically to make plans at the Harvard Club of New York. He set up an official headquarters on Wall Street and sent out fifteen thousand invitations to the right people, inviting them to join in Wood's growing number of summer encampments. Roosevelt's second son, Archibald, commonly known as Archie, was one of those who accepted.

2. Representative Swagart Shirley, quoted in ibid., 57.

In the summer of 1915, Wood picked up another idea, this one reportedly suggested by Roosevelt's oldest son, Theodore Jr. In addition to college students, Roosevelt suggested, young businessmen might also provide a lucrative source of future officers. Confined as they were to their desks in Manhattan, many of them, himself included, might find it refreshing to spend a few weeks a year in hard training. Bonding, exercise, and a change of scenery—all could have an appeal. The idea received an overwhelming response, and it soon picked up the nickname of "Tired Businessmen." No labor unions, however, were invited to participate.

To conduct this training, Wood selected an area near Plattsburg, New York, on Lake Champlain. The location had the appeal of history: a critical battle of the War of 1812 had been fought there. It possessed a more practical advantage, however. It lay within a reasonable distance from New York, but it was far enough away from the city to prevent tempting any trainee to sneak into the office. As commander of most of the Army's troops, Wood had no difficulty in securing an adequate Regular Army cadre. Thus was born the Plattsburg Movement.

Wood worked rapidly, and by the late summer of 1915 all preparations were complete. On August 9, thirteen hundred young men departed by train from New York for Wood's camp. A few, it was reported, traveled in private automobiles, and humorists quipped that some students even brought their valets with them. If those stories were true, they were quickly dispelled. Everyone, including the thirty–five–year–old mayor of New York, John Purroy Mitchel, and Charles H. Brent, Episcopal bishop of Rochester, was treated alike.[3] To Archie Roosevelt, the setup had a pleasant aspect. As an outstanding student of the previous college classes, he had been selected as one of the Plattsburg instructors. Among his students was his older brother Theodore Jr., who Archie at least felt had always lorded his family seniority a bit above him.

The supervision of the training was intense. For these thirteen hundred men, there were two hundred instructors, and Wood himself was on the spot, directing the training in person. The workdays were long. The result was a group of young men with a modicum of military training but more important a group of zealots. Two days after the first class graduated on August 25, another class came in. The Plattsburg Program was established.

Ironically, Wood's moment of triumph saw the beginning of his downfall in the eyes of President Woodrow Wilson. To attend the graduation ceremonies

3. Ibid., 66.

on that August 25, 1915, Wood invited a distinguished guest list that included President Woodrow Wilson, former president William H. Taft, and former president Theodore Roosevelt. Wilson, who had always considered the Plattsburg Movement as somewhat at odds with his policy of neutrality, sniffingly refused via a secretary. Taft politely declined.

But not Theodore Roosevelt. The "Colonel," as Roosevelt preferred to be called, appeared on the scene wearing the broad hat of the Rough Riders and in a quasi–military uniform. Concerned that some of his remarks might cause embarrassment to Wood, he asked that the graduation ceremony take place off–post, that attendance be strictly voluntary, and that the audience wear civilian clothes. Wood was able to meet these conditions. Roosevelt also showed Wood the text of the speech he planned to make. Wood requested some deletions, and Roosevelt readily accepted them.[4]

The audience that day consisted of five thousand people, taking in every word seriously. Roosevelt praised the graduating volunteers, emphasizing their courage. But then he added a telling point, that "courage stood for naught without a strong army and navy." He condemned neutrality and condemned pacifists. Brave men hate war, he said, but they hate injustice and aggression (meaning the German invasion of France) even more. He wound up with an exhortation for preparedness.

The cheers were loud and long—there were few Wilsonian neutralists in that audience—and all might have been well had it ended there. When Roosevelt went to the train station, however, he encountered reporters. There he revealed what he had deleted from his original draft. Particularly offensive to President Wilson, understandably, was Roosevelt's comparing presidents. Lincoln, he said, deserved loyalty; Buchanan did not. He went on to say that if Buchanan had been in Lincoln's position, the Union would have perished. The comparison to Wilson, while not by name, could not be lost.[5]

When the news reached President Wilson, he was predictably furious. He was also unfair. Overlooking the fact that he himself had refused Wood's invitation to attend, and that Taft had done the same, he blamed Wood for Roosevelt's transgressions. He directed Secretary Garrison to deliver a public rebuke to Wood, which Garrison did with zeal. Wood answered with a terse "Yours received, and the policies laid down will be rigidly adhered to." Roosevelt attempted to come to Wood's rescue by making a public statement: "I am, of course, responsible for the whole speech."[6] Hugh Scott, chief

4. Patricia O'Toole, *When Trumpets Call: Theodore Roosevelt after the White House*, 286.
5. Ibid., 287.
6. Hagedorn, *Leonard Wood, a Biography*, 2:166.

of staff, assured Wilson, "I am out for national preparedness and I am going to get it."

Roosevelt and Wood have been given credit for being the leaders in the so–named Preparedness Movement. To a large extent, that credit is justified, for they were the Jeremiads, the voices crying in the wilderness, who pointed out the dangers in the world war while the rest of America slept. Nevertheless, the power to implement measures for preparedness lay in other hands, in the president and in Congress. And in those two power centers, all was confusion.

Although the Constitution gives Congress certain powers, it is unclear in defining specific responsibilities. It names the president as the commander in chief, but gives Congress the power to raise armies and navies—which means money. With so many factions constituting the Congress, that body must of necessity look to the president for guidance. If the president and his advisers cannot come up with a single coordinated plan for a defense posture, how can Congress be expected to do so? That is the situation that prevailed in the first term of the presidency of Woodrow Wilson.

President Wilson's resistance to a buildup of the Army had softened during the year 1915. In his State of the Union address of 1914, he had gone out of his way to taunt those who saw danger to the United States in the European war, but the sinking of the *Lusitania* in May 1915—or, rather, the public reaction to the sinking—illustrated to him that for political reasons if for no other, he must make moves to provide for the public safety. He still had a long ways to go, however, before he could reach the views of the movement—Roosevelt, Root, Wood, and others, even his own secretary of war, Lindley Garrison. In July 1915, however, he directed Garrison to come up with a national defense plan. Garrison accordingly called on the General Staff to produce such a document.

Garrison's task was not an easy one, because viewpoints differed between the General Staff (including a large part of the Army War College); the technical services, who together still formed a significant bloc; and the National Guard, which was held in contempt by the regulars but possessed great political power. And views differed as to the purpose of a defense buildup. Would a larger army and reserve be designed for use in Europe or merely to defend the United States against a foreign landing on its shores?

Wilson had his own ideas, though he did not present them to his administration. Like others who did not expect to send an expeditionary force to Europe, he tended to favor the Navy's views over those of the Army. The Navy was not only a first line of defense but practically the only defense. His inclination was enhanced on August 20, 1915, when a German U–boat sank a British ship, the *Arabic*, with the loss of a few American lives. The American public was again so aroused that the German kaiser gave way to Wilson's demand and promised to cease submarine warfare against merchant ships. The prospect of war against Germany now seemed even more remote.

Garrison rendered his report, and on November 4, 1915, at a dinner celebrating the fiftieth anniversary of the Manhattan Club, Wilson announced the general outlines of his defense plan. Its essence was simple and general. The Regular Army was to be enlarged to 140,000 men, enough to protect American shores. Essential reliance was to be on the concept called the Continental Army, a reserve force of 400,000 men. His plan called for building battleships to bring the United States Navy up to the equivalent of the Royal Navy by the year 1920. Having announced his plan, Wilson set out on a speaking tour around the country to sell it.

Unfortunately for Wilson's program, it ran into opposition in Congress, led by the ubiquitous Representative James Hay of Virginia. Hay's arguments were complicated, but one was personal. Because Lindley Garrison was supporting the administration, Hay, who hated Garrison (and vice versa), refused to sign on. Instead of a Continental Army, Hay insisted on creating a reserve from a partially federalized National Guard.

Wilson, forced to break the impasse, declared that he would not oppose Hay's idea. Overruled by the president he served, Garrison resigned in anger. When Wilson chose as Garrison's successor a pacifist, Newton D. Baker, the proponents saw the chances of their cause as bleak. But they kept on.

Finally, on June 3, 1916, Congress passed the National Defense Act of 1916. Among other provisions, the act authorized a Regular Army of 175,000 men with a National Guard reserve of 450,000 men. It established the Army Reserve Officer Training Corps, or ROTC, which had been begun already by Leonard Wood and his supporters. A critical provision was that of authorizing the president to "federalize" the National Guard in times of emergency.

This was not a defense establishment that could fight in the European war; when war came less than a year later, its provisions had not yet even been implemented. But the framework had been set. The man given the most credit for writing the act was, ironically, none other than Representative James Hay himself.

17

On the Shelf

In March 1916, Theodore Roosevelt met with a group of friends, all Republicans, in New York City. The purpose was to discuss the presidential campaign of 1916. Among the group were Elihu Root, Henry Cabot Lodge, and Leonard Wood. A secondary purpose of the meeting was to mend fences between former comrades, especially between Roosevelt and Root who, as a member of the Taft administration, had felt obligated to help deny his former chief the Republican nomination in 1912. That reconciliation was easily accomplished.

The one man who was out of place in this group of politicians was Wood, who was still on duty as a professional Army officer. His presence, however, was not a mere oversight. It indicated Wood's growing impatience with trying to push his preparedness campaign through proper channels. Further, Wood was apparently succumbing to the presidential bug himself. Little resulted from the meeting, but the next day Roosevelt, meeting with a reporter from the *Chicago Tribune,* was quoted as being willing to support a man "who has indomitable courage, who believes fervently in the ideals of Americanism, who interprets America in forms of nationalism, and who believes that in a democracy every citizen owes his first duty to the state, and that it is necessary in the best interests and greatest happiness of the whole people that individual liberty shall at times be subservient to the greater cause of national liberty."[1] This piece of political bombast was standard stuff. It was interesting not for its contents, but for its reception. Roosevelt was apparently describing himself, but both the reporter and Wood presumed that he was talking about Wood.

1. McCallum, *Leonard Wood,* 266.

Further evidence of political proclivities on Wood's part appeared a few weeks later. He attended a great parade in New York designed to support preparedness. It was led by Edith Roosevelt herself, and it involved 125,000 participants. Despite the implied criticism of Wilson's cautious foreign policy, Wood viewed the ceremony in a prominent position, standing next to Mayor John Purroy Mitchel, a Plattsburg graduate who was a leader in the movement.

Based on these developments, President Wilson now concluded that Wood had to be removed from the political catbird's seat that New York provided. He instructed the new secretary of war, Newton D. Baker, to break the Army's Eastern Department into three parts, the Department of the Northeast (Boston), the Department of the East (New York), and the Department of the South (Charleston). Wood was offered the command of the Department of the South, but none other (except for the Army command in either Hawaii or the Philippines). He chose Charleston, especially as he had a feeling that Wilson would have preferred to get him out of the country. He was not going to comply.[2]

Wood's transfer to the command at Charleston nearly coincided with the American declaration of war against Germany on April 6, 1917. He did not, therefore, expect to remain long at this new post; the country was now in a state of flux, and officers were being moved between positions on a daily basis. Besides, Charleston was a desirable spot.

At about the time of the Roosevelt meeting in New York, an event was transpiring in far–off New Mexico that was destined to have a dramatic effect on Roosevelt and Wood. In the early–morning hours of March 9, 1916, Francisco (Pancho) Villa, the onetime Mexican general who was now reduced to the status of a bandit, crossed the border from Sonora into New Mexico and burned part of the small town of Columbus, at the edge of which stood Camp Furlong, the home of the 13th Cavalry. In Villa's raid, seventeen Americans were killed. Villa's raiding party suffered far heavier casualties, but that fact did nothing to placate an aroused American populace. Public opinion demanded retribution, and a reluctant President Wilson, for political purposes unwilling to appear "weak," ordered Brigadier General John J. Pershing, at El Paso, to organize an expedition to pursue Villa into the Mexican state of Chihuahua. Pershing's force crossed southward in two columns, one from Culberson's Ranch and the other from Columbus itself. It eventually grew to comprise ten thousand men.

2. Ibid., 267.

The selection of Pershing to command the Punitive Expedition, as it was officially called, was far from automatic. Because the force would involve a major portion of the Army's mobile strength, it was a prestigious command, coveted by several high-ranking officers. One such candidate was Major General Frederick Funston, Pershing's immediate superior as the commander of the Department of the Southwest, at San Antonio. Funston was a feisty little rooster, who because of his feat in capturing the Philippine rebel Emilio Aguinaldo fifteen years earlier was generally considered to be the Army's leading combat soldier. His great asset was his aggressiveness; his drawback was his explosive nature. As in his public support of Smith and Waller in Samar, he held brown people in contempt. Therefore, because leading a force invading foreign soil was expected to be a delicate matter, Baker set his name aside.

Wood could have been another candidate, and his cause was supported by the Army chief of staff, Hugh Scott, his former subordinate. But Wood was currently in the midst of his difficulties in Washington, and his possibility as a Republican presidential candidate was showing. So he too was passed over, and Baker selected Pershing. The order that Baker sent to San Antonio, therefore, was unusual in that it directed a commander in charge of a region of which subordinate to send. He specified Pershing by name.

What all this meant was that Pershing, though still only a brigadier general, had been elevated to a place among the top leaders of the Army. He was now a man who might be considered to command whatever expeditionary force might be sent anywhere in case of a major war.

Pershing's campaign turned out to be far more aggressive than Wilson had ever intended. One of his columns reached Parras, a town 500 miles below the border between the two countries. And it soon became apparent that the Carranza government was his real opponent, not Villa. Wilson, refusing to admit defeat, ordered Pershing to move into a semipermanent camp at Casa Grande, about 150 miles south of Columbus. There he put his force through a rigorous training program. Denied the authority to seize the city of Chihuahua, he settled down, awaiting orders on what to do next.

With Pershing in a safe encampment, the public turned its attention to the Republican National Convention in Chicago. Despite his personal fiasco in 1912, Roosevelt decided to run for the nomination again in 1916. In addition to his natural ambition, he was convinced that the country was on the road to disgrace and that he was the only man who could prevent a coming disaster. His hatred of Woodrow Wilson had grown. In 1913 he wrote to Henry Cabot Lodge, "I regard Wilson with contemptuous dislike. He has ability of a certain kind, and he has the nerve that his type so often shows in civil and domestic affairs where there is not danger of physical violence. He will jump up and down on cheap politicians, and bully and cajole men in public life who are not anxious to part company with their political chief. But he is a ridiculous creature in international matters. He is a narrow and bitter partisan, and he is intellectually thoroughly dishonest."[3]

However, Roosevelt was careful to confine such intemperate observations to close confidants. In public his complaints took on a more impersonal tone. And his opinion of the Republicans was also something short of favorable. "The Republicans are a sordid lot," he wrote to a friend. Admittedly, they were a trifle better than the Democrats, whom he called "corrupt and lunatic wild asses," and Wilson "that astute, unprincipled, and physically cowardly demagogue." But the Republicans, to him, were still a "sorry lot."[4]

Roosevelt's first problem, however, was to reinstate himself as a Republican. Attacking the Democrats could come later. Unfortunately for him, the views of the regular Republicans toward him were as low as his of them. The structure of the Progressive Party still existed, and that party (without his permission) had nominated him again. But Roosevelt had learned his lesson about splitting the party. His main target was Wilson, and to split the Republicans and Progressives again would make Wilson's reelection inevitable. So Roosevelt's only chance, a slim one, was to engineer a reunification between the Progressives and the Republicans. He hoped that his own personal popularity, which was infinitely stronger than that of any of his rivals, might overcome the still smoldering anger of the regulars. In search of victory, the Republicans might bury the hatchet and accept him back.

The loyal members of the Progressive Party agreed with Roosevelt's assessments, and they came up with an ingenious scheme. They planned to hold their presidential convention in Chicago concurrently with that of the Republicans. There, while all the excitement and confusion common to all conventions was going on, the party leaders could meet and agree on reunifying—with Theodore Roosevelt as the nominee, of course. While these negotiations were in progress, Roosevelt himself would remain in the background.

It did not work. The Republican Party leaders were not in a forgiving mood. They refused the overtures of the Progressives and went on to nominate the dignified jurist Charles Evans Hughes, and went down to a resounding defeat.

Roosevelt was furious, and in his letters he showed no lessening in his invective toward all his political rivals. But he had learned his lesson. He re-

3. Brands, *T. R.*, 735.
4. Ibid., 773.

fused the renewed nomination of the Progressive Party and took the stump campaigning for Hughes. Roosevelt's age was only fifty–eight, and he did not admit that his political career was over.

Leonard Wood's warnings of America's military weakness were nothing new. The question remained, however, as to how important that weakness was. Political leaders had to decide how much time, effort, and expense should be poured into building an army and navy that might never fight. While Americans were debating this issue, the Germans were watching. The tumult on the American scene emboldened Kaiser Wilhelm II and his advisers to underestimate America and to reconsider the wisdom of continuing to respect Woodrow Wilson's stringent demands for restricting submarine warfare. As it was, that policy was crippling one of Germany's most potent weapons, the U–boat.

On January 9, 1917, the kaiser summoned his top military advisers to his headquarters in northern Silesia. Field Marshal Paul von Hindenburg and General Erich Ludendorff, the de facto dictators of Germany, headed the list of high–ranking participants. Admiral Henning von Holtzendorff represented the naval delegation. Chancellor Theobald Bethmann–Hollweg represented the German Reichstag.

The agenda of the group was limited to one issue: whether to reopen unrestricted submarine warfare in the hope of starving Britain out of the war. The military situation on the western front had settled into a bloody stalemate, and the British naval blockade was causing great suffering in Germany. Time, they realized, was not on the German side, but increased submarine activity could possibly hasten a German victory. That hope was reinforced by the fact that the Europeans, including the British, had suffered a bad harvest in 1916, increasing Britain's vulnerability to submarine blockade.

It was agreed that the move would entail a high degree of risk of bringing America into the war. But how important was that consideration? The consensus was that such a danger had been diminished since the kaiser had made his agreement with Wilson. In the nearly two and a half years since the beginning of the European conflict, the Americans had done little to arm themselves. Their Regular Army and National Guard amounted to only a small fraction of a European army. And the Americans lacked a merchant marine, so necessary for carrying troops. American potential could not be realized, they concluded, for quite some time.

The strongest advocate of resuming unrestricted submarine warfare was Admiral Holtzendorff, who gave categorical assurances that his submarines could take Britain out of the war within six months. Hindenburg and Ludendorff largely supported him. Bethmann–Hollweg, on the other hand, harbored doubts as to its effect on Germany's political standing. The kaiser agreed with him. In the end, the views of Hindenburg and Ludendorff prevailed, and the final decision was to go ahead.

On February 1, 1917, the German ambassador to the United States, Count Johann von Bernsdorff, received instructions to inform the State Department of Germany's intentions. Bernsdorff was devastated. He was a popular man in town, and he was embarrassed but had to comply. Although he did everything possible to ease the blow, Bernsdorff knew that this move made US entry into the war practically inevitable.

And so it did. Two days after receiving the word from Germany, President Woodrow Wilson went before Congress to announce that he was breaking diplomatic relations with Imperial Germany. He did not ask for a declaration of war quite yet; he would, he declared, await an overt act on Germany's part before taking the final, tragic, step.

At that point, it was obvious that war was in the offing, and the urgency increased when on February 25, the British government in London came up with a remarkable telegraphic message from the Germans that the famous "Room Forty" had recently deciphered. The communication, which came to be called the "Zimmermann Telegram," had been addressed to the German ambassador in Mexico. Its author was the German foreign minister, Arthur Zimmermann, and it instructed his envoy to make an offer to the Mexican government. In exchange for Mexico's alliance in a war against the United States, Germany would restore all the lands the Americans had wrested from them nearly seventy years earlier in the Mexican–American War. The territory included the entire American Southwest. The offer was patently ridiculous. The prospects of Germany's ability to attack the United States and take possession of those lands were of course remote. Nevertheless, when the contents of the Zimmermann Telegram reached the American public, the indignation caused so much resentment as to constitute practically a casus belli in itself.

Another blow also fell, the sinking of a couple of British ships, one of which was the *Celtic,* with American lives lost. Wilson's ambivalence was now gone. He addressed Congress on April 2, 1917, requesting a declaration of war. The members were of the same mind, and on April 6 the United States was at war with Germany.

During those two previous months of suspended animation, President Wilson and Secretary of War Newton D. Baker had wrestled with the question of choosing the man to command any expedition the United States might send overseas—in the event that an expedition would be sent. Even if a ground force were not to be sent, a field commander had to be selected, for whatever purpose.

Up to the middle of February, such selection had not been seen as a problem. In spite of the seniority of Wood and others, the Army's leading field commander was considered to be Major General Frederick Funston, the hero of the Philippine War.[5] Funston was not known for his tact, but since the role of the Army was fighting, not diplomacy, he was assumed to be the man to command any American troops called on to fight.

That assumption came to an abrupt end, however, on the evening of February 17, 1917. Word came in to the War Department that Funston had died of a heart attack while attending a social event at the St. Anthony Hotel in San Antonio. Major Douglas MacArthur, on duty at Army headquarters that evening, took the alarming news to a party at which both Wilson and Baker were enjoying themselves. The party immediately broke up.[6]

As Wilson and Baker surveyed the field of candidates for the position, they discovered that there were few senior officers from which to pick. Major General J. Franklin Bell, a previous chief of staff, was reaching the advanced age of sixty–four. Hugh Scott, the current chief of staff, had no interest. The choice therefore really came down to one between Leonard Wood and Pershing.

Scott, himself eliminated, had views as to who else should go, and he proved to be the key figure in easing the decision. His first choice had originally been Leonard Wood. As time had gone on, however, Scott had become aware of Wood's political activities, exacerbated by his being too visibly friendly with the intemperate Roosevelt. During the years, Scott had periodically warned Wood to avoid political statements; they did not mix with a military career. Giving up on Wood on that account, Scott had finally concluded that Pershing was the man, and he made his views known to Baker and Wilson.

In retrospect, Wood's prospects for the coveted appointment were probably chimerical, because Wilson's animosity against him was too great. Wilson had, in fact, overruled Scott's recommendation that Wood be appointed to command a punitive expedition into Mexico in 1915, the expedition that never happened. But Wilson preferred not to take the political onus of the

5. When it came time to send American troops to Veracruz in 1914, for example, it had been Funston who had commanded the Army troops.

6. Writing his memoirs nearly fifty years later, MacArthur claimed that Wilson and Baker had solicited his views just after delivering the message to the gathering. There is no confirmation of that claim other than the general's own memory.

choice on himself overtly. Wood was still a popular figure among the public, so he ostensibly turned over the decision to Secretary of War Baker.

Baker at first had his doubts about Pershing as well as Wood. While leading the Punitive Expedition in Mexico, Pershing was supposedly heard criticizing President Wilson for his lukewarm support of that effort. Doubtless, considering the lack of guidance he had received from Washington, Pershing probably had made some complaint, but he was basically loyal to Wilson and was shocked when Scott advised him to mend his fences in a hurry. Pershing wrote a letter to Scott that satisfied Baker. Baker thereupon appointed Pershing to head any American expedition, although the exact nature of his mission was still unclear.[7]

Wood received the news of Pershing's appointment shortly after arriving at Charleston. He showed little emotion—he had perhaps held no hopes to receive the appointment himself. In the meantime, he was assuming a new command, which still contained the bulk of the Army. He set out on a tour of the various stations within his area. He was still immensely popular with the people in the South and was honored and feted, a fact that probably took his mind off his recent rejection.

Wood did, however, retain some hope for a future assignment overseas. He had confidence that Pershing, for whom he had performed significant favors, would stick by him. In the meantime, he still had plenty to occupy his mind.

The selection of Pershing over Wood to command the American Expeditionary Force (AEF) was simple compared to contending with former president Theodore Roosevelt and his determination to raise a volunteer division for service in whatever fighting the country faced. Although Roosevelt's hope had never been seriously considered by Wilson, Garrison, or Baker, it had been a sort of running sore for years, especially since the day the *Lusitania* had been torpedoed. In 1915 the idea had been relatively easy to shunt aside, because Wilson had no intention then of going to war. But when Wilson had broken relations with Germany in early–February 1917, Roosevelt had sent an urgent message to Baker, advising that he and his wife would cancel a vacation in the Caribbean if war became imminent. Baker answered dryly that the colonel should go ahead with his vacation, that

7. After the end of the war, Baker was asked the reason for his decision. He disclaimed personal animosity and justified his decision on the basis of Wood's alleged poor physical condition. Wood still had a slight limp as the result of his benign brain tumor.

everything was under control with regard to war preparations. Roosevelt canceled his trip anyway.

Still, even though he was now cast in the role of a supplicant, Roosevelt could not restrain himself from criticizing Wilson's delay in asking for a declaration of war. In the middle of March, he spoke to the Union League Club in New York, declaiming that the United States was already at war with Germany. Referring to old wounds such as Wilson's payment of twenty–five million dollars to Colombia as reparations for America's encouragement of Panamanian independence, he recalled the American defiance of the Barbary pirates in the early nineteenth century: "Millions for defense; not a single cent for tribute." Roosevelt translated Wilson's current attitude: "Millions for tribute but not a cent for defense." The only concession Roosevelt made in his rousing talk was to avoid using Wilson's name. Nobody was fooled.

On April 2, two weeks after Roosevelt's diatribe, Wilson's request for a declaration of war caused Roosevelt to soften his caustic criticism of Wilson. The old Rough Rider swallowed his pride, took hat in hand, and requested an audience at the White House with the man he had recently so detested. Wilson, though unenthusiastic at the prospect, felt obligated to receive a former president. Roosevelt walked through the familiar portals of his onetime home on April 10, four days after Wilson had signed the declaration of war.[8]

Not surprisingly, the meeting, therefore, started out coldly. But Roosevelt was capable of turning on the charm, and he went all out. He dismissed his previous attacks on Wilson by saying that his words were already dust. He applauded Wilson's ideal of making the world safe for democracy, "if we can make it work." Roosevelt's flattery was effective, and before the twenty–five–minute meeting was over, the two men were laughing together. Wilson promised to look into the possibilities of complying with Roosevelt's request, and Roosevelt left the Oval Office believing that he had carried the day. On the way out of the White House, he stopped to speak to Wilson's appointment secretary, Joseph Tumulty. He offered to put Tumulty on his staff when the volunteer division was organized. Further, he would promise Mrs. Tumulty that he would keep her husband safe.

Wilson probably knew that his promise to "look into" Roosevelt's request was safe from ever being fulfilled, because the General Staff was vociferous in its resistance to the idea. The members had long memories; they could recall Roosevelt's constant insubordination in Cuba back in 1898. There was no

8. Roosevelt, as president, had constructed the West Wing with its Oval Office.

place for a separate unit in a force that would consist of the Regular Army, the National Guard, and a yet–to–be–organized National Army (new divisions officered by regulars but manned by draftees). The staff also recoiled at the list of regular officers Roosevelt had claimed he needed to staff the division, the cream of the Army. When asked for a recommendation, the General Staff gave a resounding no.

Roosevelt had lost his bid. Even though French premier Georges Clemenceau pleaded that Roosevelt be sent to France to bolster morale, Wilson stayed firm. Neither Roosevelt nor Wood were to participate in the war they had long been urging, the greatest war thus far fought overseas by the US Army.

Unlike Roosevelt, who had no role to play, Leonard Wood was still greatly involved with military duties, though not of the nature he would have preferred. He left Washington for Camp Funston, Kansas, in a black mood. He sensed correctly that he was the victim of a cabal that included President Wilson, Secretary Baker, and much of the regular officer corps. He also, again with some reason, believed that the American public would have preferred him, rather than Pershing, to have been named to lead the AEF in France. After all, Wood had been a national hero and Army chief of staff ten years before Pershing, in 1916, had risen to the status of one of the Army's top generals. Despite those causes for pique, Wood was resolved to do his best.

Wood's arrival at Camp Funston in August 1917 was not auspicious. The 89th was a mere training division that had not been provided with weapons, horses, or even uniforms. Nevertheless, he coped with those obstacles. He procured blue denim "fatigue" uniforms and armed his men with "rifles" shaped from pieces of wood. Though hampered by foul weather, he began to make progress in drill and discipline, but of course not marksmanship.

Welcome relief from this training assignment arrived in October 1917, after Wood had been at Camp Funston only a couple of months, when he was placed on a temporary assignment to visit France as an observer. Secretary Baker had decided to send the commanding generals of all the training divisions for a visit to the front in France. A meningitis epidemic that broke out in camp nearly upset his plans, but fortunately it abated in time for his departure.

If Baker had expected Wood to be treated by the British and French as just any other major general, he was being unrealistic. Despite his temporary incarceration at Camp Funston, Wood was still a public figure both at home and abroad, noted as a close friend of Theodore Roosevelt. The Europeans were also conscious that in that capacity, Wood had been prominent in urging American participation in the war against Germany. Wood could never be treated routinely by European authorities.

Such special treatment was quite agreeable to Wood, who had apparently no desire to be seen as just another visiting major general. He appears to have resolved to make use of the visit to induce the Allies to pressure Wilson and Baker to send him to France in some capacity or another. He would be willing, for example, to serve under Pershing but preferably not under his direct command.[9] Wood still hoped that he could change Pershing's mind about an assignment to the AEF.

Wood's first stop on his way to France was London, where he met with the chief of the Imperial Staff, Sir William Robertson, and Field Marshal Sir John French, who had commanded the British Expeditionary Force for the first year of the war. In those talks, he was less than supportive of President Wilson's policies. The American and British governments were in disagreement over the use of the American soldiers being sent to Europe. The British wanted to assign them to British units as fillers, replacements. Such a scheme was directly opposed to American official policy. Pershing, with Wilson's full backing, was exerting all efforts to establish an independent American army.

This was an emotional issue for Wilson and Pershing, who believed that an independent US Army was essential to President Wilson's position at the peace table following what was presumed to be a future Allied victory. In his discussions with the British, however, Wood compromised, offering no objection to sending some American units, perhaps battalions, to fight in British regiments. Regardless of the merits of the arguments, Wood's unauthorized statements ran against American policy. When word got out, Wood's chances for an overseas command shrank even further.

Wood did no better when he arrived in Paris on December 13, 1917. Ignoring the advice of his friends, he visited Marshal Joseph Joffre, the retired hero of the Marne, to whom he expressed much the same position as he had in Britain. He agreed that American brigades could be put into French divisions. Again, word reached Pershing, who was described as "furious."

After a couple of days in Paris, Wood visited the British forces at Ypres, Belgium, where he was friends with two of the commanders. There he was able to get a feel for the front, to experience the terror of the incoming heavy artillery rounds, something his own service in Cuba and the Philippines had not given him. Back again in France, he visited the French commander, Marshal Philippe Pétain, who was a favorite of all the Americans in France.

9. Wood's friend General Frank McCoy, for example, hoped to secure Wood a position in command of a large American formation under British command. McCallum, *Leonard Wood,* 270. Such a command was finally established as II US Corps, but not under Wood's command.

An accident then nearly brought Wood's career to a close. At the French Sixth Army School of Automatic Arms, witnessing a mortar demonstration, he was standing nearby as the French demonstrated a way to extend the range of the weapon by adding rings of cordite "accelerant." They added one too many. A shell stuck in the tube, and the mortar exploded, breaking the body of the mortar into fragments.

Wood was standing between the commandant of the school and the assistant commandant. Pieces of the mortar killed both of Wood's companions, and neither spectacle was pretty. The commandant was decapitated, and the assistant commandant was hit in the head, his brains splattered all over Wood's blouse. Wood himself was wounded in the forearm. Offered priority in evacuation, he refused, insisting that men wounded more seriously than he be evacuated first. And when vehicular transportation was not readily available, he walked a half mile to the point where he could be picked up by ambulance.[10] After a few weeks in the hospital, he recovered with little permanent damage.

Although Pershing stoutly refused to accept Leonard Wood as part of his command in France, they were onetime comrades in arms. Pershing had not completely forgotten that Wood had done him significant favors in the past. Pershing therefore invited the visitor to spend his convalescence at Pershing's headquarters, at Chaumont. But again everything went wrong. The night after Wood had visited Verdun, Pershing hosted a dinner for him. In his after–dinner talk, Wood was indiscreetly critical of Pershing himself.

That did it. Pershing canceled Wood's plans to visit London on the way back to the United States, sending him home directly by way of Bordeaux. That still did not defeat Wood. In testimony before the Senate Military Committee on March 25, he criticized certain aspects of the American war effort. From that time on, if not before, Leonard Wood gave up on working "within the system." He was now a politician in uniform. He therefore stayed around Washington for ten days, attempting to see President Wilson. During that time, he was called before a medical examining board to determine his fitness for active duty.

Pershing, now a deadly enemy in far–off France, was behind that physical examination, as a way of retiring his nemesis from the Army. To Pershing's and Baker's disappointment, however, the medical board found Wood in excellent physical condition, the only one of the nine officers being so examined who passed. Wood therefore headed back to Kansas to resume command of

10. Ibid., 271–72.

the 89th Division, which was now nearing the time for overseas deployment. But again he was frustrated. On May 22, 1918, he was removed from command of the 89th when it was at the New York port of embarkation. Pershing had had the last word.

Rightly furious at the way he had been humiliated, Wood proceeded from New York to the War Department, there to confront Secretary Baker. Public furor was high over Wood's treatment, so high that Baker would doubtless have liked to have given him command of a corps in the British sector, outside of Pershing's area. Or Wood might even be sent to command American forces in Italy. Baker's hands were tied, however. Pershing had declared that he would not have Wood in the European theater in any capacity, and because Baker had committed himself to complying with any request (or demand) that Pershing might levy, he offered Wood command of the Western Department at the Presidio of San Francisco.

Wood flatly turned that offer down. So long as he was with a division, he reasoned, there was some chance of being sent overseas before the war ended. The great Ludendorff offensives of the spring of 1918 had just begun, and the Allies might be so desperate that even the raw 10th Division, which had replaced the 89th at Funston, might be sent. After the session with Baker, Wood set out once again for Kansas, arriving in the middle of June 1918. When he did so, he was advised by Theodore Roosevelt to "contain his bitterness" and hold his tongue for the moment. All indications were that the Republicans would regain the presidency in the 1920 elections, and from then on things would be different. Wood bided his time.[11] The time never came.

11. Ibid., 274.

18

"The Old Lion Is Dead"

When Roosevelt and Wood left Washington in the summer of 1917, Wood simply stayed on duty. Roosevelt, however, resumed his campaign of fury against Woodrow Wilson, blaming the president and his administration for everything that was falling short of expectations.

He did, however, believe fervently in the cause, so if he himself was to be denied frontline duty, he set out to ensure that his family would be well represented. Two of his four sons, Theodore Jr. and Archibald, presented no problem, as they were already in service as reserve officers. But to ensure that they saw frontline service, Roosevelt approached Pershing, asking that both boys be sent overseas as privates. Pershing accepted them for service with the 1st Division, which was about to sail for France, but he gave them rank according to their reserve status. For some reason, both Ted and Archie were assigned to the 26th Infantry Regiment, Ted as a battalion commander and Archie as a platoon leader. Both were fully qualified as infantry officers.

The situation of the two younger boys was more complicated. Kermit, who had lived for years in Brazil, had a broader background than Ted or Archie, but he lacked the Plattsburg training. He therefore decided to join the British army, possibly to avoid family competition. His father approved and wrote directly to his friend British prime minister David Lloyd George. As a result, Kermit was assigned to a British unit in the Middle East. The youngest son, Quentin, decided on his own to join the fledgling Army Air Service. When he won his wings as a pursuit pilot, his father felt a particular joy. Quentin had always been the one he feared might not live up to the tradition of the Roosevelts. The boy had always been a bit overweight and by nature a prankster. Quentin had now come into his own.

Aside from making those arrangements, Roosevelt himself had no active role to play. He and Edith therefore settled down at Sagamore Hill, where he went back to his writing. At first he wrote for magazines but then settled for producing a weekly column for the *Kansas City Star,* a paper with which he had always had a close relationship. His editorials, short in accordance with the standard format of the *Star,* continued to be hostile to the Wilson administration. Roosevelt also wrote letters to various friends that were even more vitriolic. French premier Georges Clemenceau, for one, was on the receiving end of several diatribes against Roosevelt's own president.

Sitting at home with their sons in service, Roosevelt and his wife felt a natural concern for the safety of their four sons. Their father's role in putting them at the forefront of the danger did not mean that the parents were free of anxiety. To fill the time, the parents flooded their sons and their sons' families with mail.[1] Roosevelt worried when he received word that Archie had sustained a serious wound, but he beamed with pride to learn that he had been decorated by the French with the Croix de Guerre. Other than that, the Roosevelts could only sit and wait.

This was a new experience. For the first time, it is fair to say, TR was experiencing war from a new angle, that of those left behind when their loved ones march off to Danger. He was particularly solicitous for their mother. But aside from that concern, he was not particularly worried. He was happy when Quentin had written him gleefully, reporting that he thought he had shot down his first German airplane. And in July 1918, he took great pride in his son Archie's decoration.

On the sixteenth of that month, the blow struck. As Roosevelt was sitting in his library that afternoon, Phil Thompson, of the Associated Press, entered with a puzzled look on his face. He carried a garbled report from the *New York Sun* that did not give specifics but mentioned the name Roosevelt. The newspaper had instructed Thompson to "watch" Sagamore Hill.

Roosevelt knew what such a dire warning meant: something had happened to one of his boys. He took Thompson to a room outside of Edith's earshot and asked him to say nothing until they received further word. He did not know which one of the boys was in trouble, but he surmised that it had to be Quentin. He had been in close touch with all of his sons, and he knew that Archie and Ted were both in the hospital with debilitating but not life–threatening wounds. Kermit, he knew, had not yet reached Europe

1. The three older boys were all married. Quentin was engaged to a young lady much approved by both of his parents.

from the Middle East. That left only one possibility. The question now was what had happened.

Roosevelt kept his counsel. Out of consideration for Edith, he said nothing about Thompson's visit through the evening. But the next morning, Thompson returned. Quentin, he advised, had been shot down behind enemy lines on July 14—Bastille Day. His fate was as yet unknown. Roosevelt then told Edith, and together they endured the excruciating wait for news as to whether Quentin had survived. Finally, after a few days, word came in. Quentin was dead.

The death of his son Quentin stayed with Theodore Roosevelt for the rest of the short time remaining in his life. Edith suffered similarly, but her grief was not a cause for concern for her health as it was with Roosevelt. To make matters worse, his grief was exacerbated by guilt: he knew that he had personally sought to place his boys in the worst part of the battle—the frontline infantry and the fledgling Army Air Service. Clutching the fleeting concept of glory as a drowning man does a log, he told himself that even if all four of his sons had been killed, he would still have done the right thing. He took some solace in recalling his own brief service in Cuba twenty years earlier, where he had taken risks similar to theirs. In irrational moments, he blamed President Wilson for Quentin's death. Such moments, however, passed when Roosevelt realized his lack of logic.

His grief did not alter Roosevelt's contempt for President Wilson. Because Germany was totally responsible for beginning the world war, Roosevelt contended, he was appalled by Wilson's "Fourteen Points," which had been published as a means of ending the war "without victory." Only a complete, unconditional surrender on the part of Germany, Roosevelt insisted, would prevent a recurrence of the present war. History later proved him to be correct, but it was not a popular position at the time.

Meanwhile, Roosevelt's physical condition began weakening. He knew also that his age—sixty years—was considered advanced at the time. Nevertheless, he clung to the belief that he had one more fight in him. He declined suggestions that he run for governor of New York in 1920, because regaining the presidency was still on his mind. He resolved to make his one more fight for that office.

In the autumn of 1918, with the end of the world war obviously coming near, President Wilson made a grievous political error, one that demolished what was left of bipartisanship in the United States. To ease ratification of any agreements that might come out of the war, Wilson asked the country to elect a Democratic Senate and House of Representatives. The implication that great international issues were matters of partisan concern led to a rise of resentment, with the result that the Democrats were severely trounced in the 1918 congressional election. That victory at the polls gave the Republicans renewed hope for regaining the White House in 1920. The leading Republican candidate, though by no means the only one, was Roosevelt. If Roosevelt should not for some reason survive, it was reported, the man he hoped would receive the Republican nomination was Leonard Wood.[2]

On November 11, 1918, the Great War ended. Marshal Ferdinand Foch met with representatives of Germany in a railroad car in the woods of Compiègne, and they signed an agreement designed to destroy Germany's ability to carry on the fight. The terms of a long–term peace treaty would be settled in the future, but the Armistice ensured that when the statesmen gathered, Germany would be unable to resist any terms dictated by the Allies, no matter how arbitrary. The day after that news came in, Roosevelt was admitted to the hospital with a serious knee infection.

The cause of the flare–up was diagnosed as "inflammatory rheumatism," and the doctors attributed it to a recurrence of an infection Roosevelt had suffered in his near–fatal exploration of the "River of Doubt" in Brazil in 1913–14. Other causes were possible, but the important fact was that the condition was painful and debilitating, keeping the former president in the hospital for several weeks. He was allowed to return to Sagamore Hill for Christmas, well sedated with morphine, but was expected to return to the hospital when the Christmas festivities were over. At that point, nobody believed that his condition was life threatening.

The Roosevelts had a pleasant Christmas, considering the shadow cast by Quentin's death. The family noticed that the patriarch found relief in the gaiety of his grandchildren, young people who had not yet experienced the tragedy of war and who hardly remembered their uncle Quentin, if they knew him at all.

Roosevelt remained at Sagamore Hill for several days without much change in his condition. As late as Saturday, January 5, 1919, he worked hard all afternoon, writing and editing. That evening he mentioned having shortness of breath when talking with Edith, but when the doctors came by for their evening call, the old Rough Rider assured them that he was fine, a customary habit of a man who would never admit, at least to the doctors, that he was sick.

2. McCallum, *Leonard Wood*, 275.

Nevertheless, family and servants suspected that something was wrong, and they kept a close watch on the ailing Roosevelt. At 2:00 a.m., when Edith looked in on him, he seemed all right, but two hours later, James Amos, the longtime family servant who slept in the next room, did not like the way he was breathing. Amos called the trained nurse, and when she arrived all breathing had stopped.

With the nation's grief, the doctors made a statement:

> Colonel Roosevelt had been suffering from an attack of inflammatory rheumatism for about two months. His progress had been entirely satisfactory and his condition had not given cause for special concern. On Sunday he was in good spirits and spent the evening with his family, dictating letters. He retired at 11 o'clock and at 4 o'clock in the morning his manservant who occupied an adjoining room noticed that, while sleeping quietly, Colonel Roosevelt's breathing was hollow. He died almost immediately, without awakening. The cause of death was an embolus.[3]

Kermit Roosevelt was present. His message to his brothers and sisters was terse: "The Old Lion is dead."

3. Obituary of Theodore Roosevelt, *New York Times*, January 7, 1919.

19

Wood Carries On

Word of Roosevelt's unexpected death flashed across the country instantly. Wood, still at Camp Funston, received the news as he sat down to breakfast that same morning. He was not a demonstrative type, and in public he displayed little emotion, but in his diary he wrote, "Sad, sad business, all of it. I have lost my best friend."[1] He then sent the proper telegrams to the Roosevelt family and prepared for the trip back to Sagamore Hill, where he participated in all the funeral rites.

The TR–Wood partnership did not end with Roosevelt's death, however. As in life, they had worked for the same causes, so Wood resolved to continue the unfinished business of restoring the Republican Party and to defeating Woodrow Wilson's proposed League of Nations when it came up before the Senate. Wood dedicated himself to carrying on that work.

Ever since Newton D. Baker had refused to allow Wood to take the 89th Division overseas, Wood had become less and less disposed to restraining himself in the nonpolitical manner expected of Regular Army officers. And he had come to bask in the enthusiasm with which his many speeches on military preparedness were received. So encouraged, he began to conceive himself as an orator. Aware of the widespread public resentment against Baker for what was viewed as shabby treatment during the war, Wood began to see a future for himself in politics.

Up to the time of Roosevelt's death, the big obstacle to Wood's political ambitions had been his unflinching loyalty to his friend and mentor Roosevelt.

1. McCallum, *Leonard Wood,* 278.

That inhibition was now gone. He had strong rivals—Lodge, Frank Knox, Hiram Johnson, William Borah—but Roosevelt had dwarfed them. He had lived down his fiasco of 1912, and when he died he was restored to the leadership of the party. According to Wood's biographer, "Conservatives and progressives alike acclaimed [Roosevelt]; he had no rival for the nomination as the party's candidate in 1920; even his bitterest enemies had taken the journey to Canossa. It seemed inevitable that he should take up the leadership in the work of construction, which the President had relinquished by default. But on January 6, Roosevelt had died."[2]

Talk of Wood's assuming the mantle of Roosevelt's leadership began before TR's funeral ceremonies at Oyster Bay. Between eulogies to their fallen hero, politicians were looking at Wood as the key to the future. Wood later claimed that even some members of the Roosevelt family had mentioned the possibility to him.[3] Many people agreed.

With the war over, Wood's military duties were far from strenuous, and he was afforded time to accept speaking engagements all over the country, receiving honorary degrees from at least three universities. He made use of these events to criticize the administration. He had his own style. As described in the *Chicago Daily Tribune*, his stump speech was

> twelve minutes of detached granite. He tramped in, he stood up and clasped his hands behind his stocky body. He said about a columnful and then he tramped out, grizzled, ruddy, stalwart, he stood square and he talked square. No flowing periods. No gestures. A whimsical flicker of a smile and a burly half bow. The level voice hammered out grim sentences. Not a flicker of emotion crossed the oak-hewn face. He began; he said something; he finished, "Good day." He marched out. It was like a rite, this time when the audience rose and stood until he disappeared.[4]

In the middle of February 1919, Wood left Camp Funston and took over the Army's Central Command, with headquarters in Chicago. A couple of days later, in Kansas City, he nearly overstepped himself. Before an audience

2. Hagedorn, *Leonard Wood, a Biography,* 2:326. The term *journey to Canossa* signifies an act of penance or submission. It is based on a long and dangerous trek made by Holy Roman Emperor Henry IV over the Alps in 1077 to the fortress of Canossa, in Tuscany. When Henry arrived, Pope Gregory VII, after some delay, lifted Henry's excommunication, which he had levied over a dispute over appointment of church clergy.

3. McCallum, *Leonard Wood,* 276.

4. Ibid., 275–76.

of twenty thousand people, he parlayed a ceremony honoring the memory of Roosevelt into an attack on Wilson. The audience roared its approval, not particularly worried about whether the insertion of partisan politics was in the best of taste.

Wood's political sales point depended on his being viewed as Roosevelt's successor. To that end, then, he made full use of such TR language as "bully" and "Speak softly and carry a big stick." But in spite of the calculated rhetoric, he lacked Roosevelt's real feel for the common man. He was not a true "progressive" like Roosevelt, and he had no zeal for issues such as the banning of child labor, old–age pensions, and decent workweeks. Instead, he concentrated on taking advantage of a growing public fear of Bolshevism—the "Red Scare." Law and order took precedence over humanitarian issues. He presented himself as the man who would protect the public, even wearing military uniform while making political speeches. Authoritarian rule, he at least hinted, was the way of keeping the public safe. The role of government was not public welfare; it was to afford a safe environment for industry to thrive on its own.

For a while, the rudimentary political polls of the time gave Wood a slight lead over the other candidates. But the polls were misleading, in a way, because nobody had a clear, decisive lead. Out of the five foremost Republican candidates—in order, Wood, Governor Frank Lowden of Illinois, Senator Hiram Johnson of California, Herbert Hoover, and Senator Warren Harding of Ohio—Wood never attained more than 17 percent of the vote. Although he was more popular personally than his principal rival, Governor Lowden, their counts were only a percentage point different.

The Republican National Convention was to be held in mid–1920, and that timing was disadvantageous to Wood's cause. Eighteen months had passed since Roosevelt's death, too long for Wood to continue his image as TR's successor. And his pose as the nation's protector proved ephemeral. At the beginning of 1920, at the time when Wood formally announced his candidacy, the Red Scare was in full swing. But by June, the issue had lost its appeal. The public's fear had eased, and with it the value of the Red Scare as a political issue. So Wood was forced to tone down his most telling strong point.

Other matters threatened Wood's position. One was dissension among his staff. His first campaign manager, John T. King, was a shrewd political strategist who recognized Wood's naïveté and urged him to remain largely in the background.[5] And like Winfield Scott in 1852, Wood ignored the advice—and

5. The same advice had been given back in 1852 to another military hero–turned–politician, Winfield Scott.

lost to a nonentity. King finally became discouraged and resigned from Wood's team, replaced by William C. Proctor, an oilman and political amateur.

Wood must, however, be given credit for integrity in the political process. One day he was approached by a Kansas oil magnate, "Big Jake" Hamon, who guaranteed that he would ensure Wood's nomination in exchange for assurances of being appointed secretary of the interior. Wood, who saw this offer as blatant bribery, ordered Hamon out of the office, thus destroying his best chance of winning the nomination. Both Hamon and the disillusioned John King joined the plot to promote a man they knew they could rule, Senator Warren G. Harding.

In June 1920, when the convention opened in Chicago, Wood's name still led the pack, but not by much. For several ballots, the two front runners, Wood and Lowden, seesawed back and forth in the lead. Finally, after much negotiating in many of the proverbial smoke-filled rooms, Wood's and Lowden's names both dropped out of sight. The convention finally nominated Warren Harding by acclamation.

Although Wood's concession speech was gracious—his demeanor was called by some his finest moment—he was personally infuriated over what he considered a plot against him. His feeling of victimization had some justification. But on the whole, it was Wood himself, with his political ineptitude, that brought about his defeat. That failure came about at least partly through his abandonment of the basic political principles of his old partner, Theodore Roosevelt.

The presidential election of November 1920 went as foreseen, and Republican senator Warren G. Harding easily won the White House over Democrat James M. Cox. But once in office, Harding still felt uneasy about Wood, who remained both popular and outspoken. A little more than a year after Harding's inauguration, the problem was solved when Wood retired from the Army by reaching statutory age. On entering civilian life, he was inundated with various job offers, one of which was the presidency of the University of Pennsylvania. Finally, however, Harding induced his potential troublemaker to return to the Philippines in a civilian capacity, first as the head of a commission to investigate affairs and then to take over as governor-general. Wood finally accepted.

Wood spent the remaining seven years of his life as governor-general. They were not a happy time. He was out of sympathy with the aspirations of the Filipinos for immediate independence, and he used his power of veto frequently to nullify measures of the Philippine Assembly. At one point, one of his vetoes was appealed to President Calvin Coolidge, who succeeded when Harding died in office. Coolidge supported Wood.

During those years, Wood's personal life was difficult. His two sons, both of whom began their careers as Army officers, left service to speculate in the oil business; both came to disaster. Even more disturbing was the degeneration in Wood's physical condition. The brain tumor that for years had caused him to limp came back in force, and toward the end of his time in the Philippines he was forced to resort to ruses to hide his condition. Finally, in 1927, he left his post in Manila and returned for consultations and surgery with his old doctor, Harvey Cushing.

This time even Cushing's skilled surgery was not successful. Leonard Wood died at Boston on August 7, 1927.

Epilogue

They were two ambitious, driving men, nearly obsessed with power, both personal and national. Oddly, Theodore Roosevelt, a master politician, fancied himself a soldier. Leonard Wood, a great soldier and administrator, flirted with the idea he had political talents as well.

Both were wrong. TR would have been a disaster as a regular officer; Wood, who inherited Roosevelt's delegates at the Republican National Convention of 1920, was never taken seriously. They were extremely different personalities: the gregarious, outgoing Roosevelt and the more aloof Wood. But their talents supplemented each other, with results that have put the nation in their debt.

Their most important achievement came in the years just preceding America's entry into the Great War. At the Plattsburg training camp, and others, they began to plant the seeds for training an officer corps, so essential to a fighting force at a time when military preparedness was not only unsupported but viewed with hostility by President Woodrow Wilson.

Their other great accomplishment was the recasting of the Army staff, on paper by President Roosevelt in 1904, and by Leonard Wood as chief of staff in the Taft administration.

Yet despite these stellar accomplishments, they would have been forgotten were it not for their creditable but relatively unimportant day in the Cuban campaign of 1898 when they charged up San Juan (Kettle) Hill on July 1. The "Rough Riders of San Juan Hill" will always be their claim to fame.

That fact is ironic. One is reminded of the limerick by the humorist Edward Lear:

> A goddess capricious is Fame
> You may strive to make noted your name.
> But she either neglects you
> Or cruelly selects you
> For laurels distinct from your aim.

Appendix A

Order of Battle

Organization, Fifth Corps
July 1, 1898
Major General William Shafter[1]

1st Division MG Jacob L. Kent

Hawkins's Brigade: 6th Inf, 16th Inf, 71st NY Vol Inf
Pearson's Brigade: 2d Inf, 21st Inf, 10th Cav
Wickoff's Brigade: 13th Inf, 24th Inf, 9th Cav

2d Division MG William Lawton

Chaffee's Brigade: 8th Inf, 22d Inf, 2d Mass Vol Inf
Ludlow's Brigade: 1st, 4th, 25th Inf
Miles's Brigade: 7th, 12th, 17th Inf

Cavalry Division (dismounted) BG S. S. Sumner (Wheeler)

Sumner's Brigade: 3 regular cavalry regiments
Wood's Brigade (Young): 10th Cav, 1st Cav, 1st Vol Cav

Independent Brigade BG J. C. Bates

2 infantry regiments, 1 cavalry squadron

1. Dierks, *Leap to Arms,* 86–87.

Appendix B

Timeline, Philippines, 1901-1906

July 4, 1901	President McKinley establishes Philippine Committee
July 4, 1901 to July 4, 1902	Taft Commission and Philippine Division, USA, govern separate areas, depending on hostility
September 17, 1901	Theodore Roosevelt succeeds to the presidency on McKinley assassination.
September 28, 1901	BG Jake Smith massacre at Balangiga, Samar
Late 1901	Captain Pershing reports to Manila.
November, 1901	Pershing sent from Manila to Iligan, Mindanao.
February, 1902	General Nelson Miles unsuccessfully proposes himself to be governor of the Philippines.
April, 1902	Pershing transferred to Camp Vicars, Lake Lanao.
July 4, 1902	United States signs peace treaty with Insurrectos.
June 22, 1903	NYT carries story of Pershing's battle at Bacolod.

End of July, 1903	Pershing leaves PI.
February 8, 1904	Russo-Japanese War. Japan victorious, 1905.
1905	Commissioner of PI becomes governor general.
February, 1906	Leonard Wood perpetrates Mount Dajo massacre. President Roosevelt hastily congratulates him.

Bibliography

Amchan, Arthur. *The Most Famous Soldier in America: A Biography of Lt. Gen. Nelson A. Miles, 1839-1925.* Alexandria, VA: Amchan, 1989.

Auchincloss, Louis. *Theodore Roosevelt.* The American Presidents. New York: Times Books, 2002.

Beale, Howard K. *Theodore Roosevelt and the Rise of America to World Power.* Baltimore: Johns Hopkins University Press, 1956.

Brands, H. W., ed. *The Selected Letters of Theodore Roosevelt.* New York: Cooper Square Press, 2001.

——. *T. R.: The Last Romantic.* New York: Basic Books, 1997.

Bruno, Thomas A. "Samar: The Violent End of Insurgency." *Army History* (Spring 2011): 30-46.

Chambers, John Whitely, II, ed. *The Oxford Companion to American Military History.* New York: Oxford University Press, 1999.

Clifford, John Garry. *The Citizen Soldiers: The Plattsburg Training Camp Movement, 1913-1920.* Lexington: University Press of Kentucky, 1972.

Clute, Penelope D. "The Plattsburg Idea." *New York Archives* (Fall 2005).

Cooper, John Milton. *The Warrior and the Priest.* Cambridge, MA: Belknap Press, 2010.

Creel, George. *The War, the World, and Wilson.* New York: Harper and Bros., 1920.

Davis, Richard Harding. *The Cuban and Puerto Rico Campaigns.* New York: Scribner and Sons, 1898.

Dierks, Jack Cameron. *A Leap to Arms: The Cuban Campaign of 1898.* Philadelphia: Lippincott, 1970.

Feuer, A. B. *The Santiago Campaign of 1898.* Westport, CT: Praeger, 1993.

Finnegan, John Patrick. *Against the Specter of a Dragon: The Campaign for American Military Preparedness, 1914-1917.* Westport, CT: Greenwood Press, 1974.

Freidel, Frank. *The Splendid Little War.* New York: Bramhall House, 1958.

Gates, John M. "Two American Wars in Asia: Successful Colonial Warfare in the Philippines and Cold War Failure in Vietnam." *War in History* 8, no. 1 (2001).

Hagedorn, Hermann. *Leonard Wood, a Biography.* 2 vols. New York: Harper and Brothers, 1931.

Harbaugh, William Henry. *Power and Responsibility: The Life and Times of Theodore Roosevelt.* New York: Farrar, Straus, and Cudahy, 1961.

Heatley, Jeff, ed. *Bully! Colonel Theodore Roosevelt, the Rough Riders, and Camp Wikoff, Montauk, New York, 1898.* New York: Pushcart Press, 1998.

Heller, Charles E., and William A. Stofft, eds. *America's First Battles.* Lawrence: University Press of Kansas, 1986.

Hobbs, William Herbert. *Leonard Wood: Administrator, Soldier, and Citizen.* New York: G. P. Putnam's Sons, 1920.

Jessup, Phillip C. *Elihu Root.* 2 vols. New York: Dodd, Mead, 1938.

Jones, Gregg R. *Honor in the Dust: Theodore Roosevelt, War in the Philippines, and the Rise and Fall of America's Imperial Dream.* New York: New American Library, 2012.

Karnow, Stanley. *In Our Image: America's Empire in the Philippines.* New York: Random House, 1989.

Kerney, James. *The Political Education of Woodrow Wilson.* New York: Century, 1926.

Koistinen, Paul A. C. *Mobilizing for Modern War.* Lawrence: University Press of Kansas, 1997.

Lane, Jack C. *Armed Progressive: General Leonard Wood.* San Rafael, CA: Presidio Press, 1978.

Leopold, Richard W. *Elihu Root and the Conservative Tradition.* Boston: Little, Brown, 1954.

Lowry, Edward G. *Washington Close-Ups: Intimate Views of Some Public Figures.* Boston: Houghton-Mifflin, 1921.

Marcosson, Isaac F. *Leonard Wood: Prophet of Preparedness.* New York: Biblio Bazaar, 1917.

McCallum, Jack. *Leonard Wood: Rough Rider, Surgeon, Architect of American Imperialism.* New York: New York University Press, 2006.

Miller, Stuart Creighton. *Benevolent Assimilation: The American Conquest of the Philippines, 1899-1903.* New Haven, CT: Yale University Press, 1982.

Minger, Ralph Eldin. *William Howard Taft and United States Foreign Policy: The Apprenticeship Years, 1900-1908.* Urbana: University of Illinois Press, 1975.

Morison, Elting E., ed. *The Letters of Theodore Roosevelt.* Cambridge, MA: Harvard University Press, 1936.

Morris, Edmund. *Colonel Roosevelt.* New York: Random House, 2010.

——. *The Rise of Theodore Roosevelt.* New York: Coward, McCann, 1979.

Norton, Aloysius A. *Theodore Roosevelt.* Boston: Twayne, 1980.

Ossad, Stephen L. "The Frustrations of Leonard Wood." *Army* (Association of the United States Army) (September 2003).

O'Toole, Patricia. *When Trumpets Call: Theodore Roosevelt after the White House.* New York: Simon and Schuster, 2005.

Parker, John H. *History of the Gatling Gun Detachment, Fifth Army Corps at Santiago.* Gloucester: Dodo Press, 2007.

Renehan, Edward J., Jr. *The Lion's Pride: Theodore Roosevelt and His Family in Peace and War.* New York: Oxford University Press, 1998.

Roosevelt, Theodore. *America and the World War: Fear God and Take Your Own Part.* New York: Scribner's Sons, 1926.

———. *An Autobiography.* New York: Charles Scribner's Sons, 1924.

———. *The Rough Riders.* New York: Charles Scribner's Sons, 1899.

Ruddy, Daniel, ed. *Theodore Roosevelt's History of the United States.* Washington, DC: Smithsonian Books, 2010.

Samuels, Peggy, and Harold Samuels. *Teddy Roosevelt at San Juan.* College Station: Texas A&M University Press, 1997.

Slayden, Ellen Maury. *Washington Wife: Journal of Ellen Maury Slayden from 1897-1919.* New York: Harper and Row, 1963.

Smith, Gene. *Until the Last Trumpet Sounds.* New York: John Wiley and Sons, 1998.

Startt, James D. *Woodrow Wilson and the Press: Prelude to the Presidency.* New York: Macmillan Palgrave, 2004.

Stimson, Harry L., and McGeorge Bundy. *On Active Service in Peace and War.* New York: Harper and Brothers, 1947.

Thomas, Evan. *The War Lovers.* Boston: Little, Brown, 2010.

Trask, David F. *The War with Spain in 1898.* The Macmillan Wars of the United States. New York: Macmillan, 1981.

Vandiver, Frank E. *Black Jack: The Life and Times of John J. Pershing.* 2 vols. College Station: Texas A&M University Press, 1977.

Walker, Dale L. *The Boys of '98: Theodore Roosevelt and the Rough Riders.* New York: Tom Dougherty Associates, 1998.

Weigley, Russell F. *History of the United States Army.* New York: Macmillan, 1967.

Wolff, Leon. *Little Brown Brother.* Garden City, NY: Doubleday, 1961.

Wood, Leonard. *Our Military History: Its Facts and Fallacies.* Chicago: Reilly and Britton, 1916.

Yockelson, Mitchell. "'I Am Entitled to the Medal of Honor and I Want It': Theodore Roosevelt and His Quest for Glory." *Prologue* (National Archives) (Spring 1998).

Acknowledgments

As always for more than twenty years, my right arm in this effort has been Mrs. Dorothy W. (Dodie) Yentz, who keeps the "official" manuscript, prepares it for final submission, and performs a myriad of other functions. My wife, Joanne, also assists as always, by providing suggestions and giving encouragement.

Friends have also helped. I would like to make special mention of the contributions of Dr. Mitchell Yockelson, of the National Archives, who is an authority on Army history in general and the author of writings on the role of Colonel Theodore Roosevelt at San Juan Hill. Mitch was particularly generous in lending me some of his valuable books for an extended period of time.

Kara Lesinski and Sylvia Graham, of the Association of Graduates, West Point, provided invaluable obituaries for deceased members of the Military Academy.

I am also indebted (in alphabetical order) to John H. (Jack) Cushman, Dorothy Daniel, David Driscoll, Kimberly Fernley, Robert H. Ferrell, Judy Haddaway, Daniel D. Holt, Beverly Jarrett, June Koch, Gerard F. McCauley, Robert and Cecelia Nobel, and Susan Strange.

Fortunately, Chris Robinson has once again been available to provide maps, also vital to a military book.

Index

About the Author

John S. D. Eisenhower is the author of many books, including *They Fought at Anzio* (University of Missouri Press), *Soldiers and Statesmen* (University of Missouri Press), *The Bitter Woods*, and Yanks. He lives in Trappe, Maryland.